Derek Tangye ha[...] world for his scr[...] farm in Cornwall. The series, which began with *A Gull on the Roof*, describes a simple way of life which thousands of his readers would like to adopt themselves.

Derek and his wife left their glamorous existence in London when they discovered Minack, a deserted cottage close to the cliffs on Mount's Bay. Jeannie gave up her job as Press Relations Officer of the Savoy Hotel Group and Derek Tangye resigned from MI5. They then proceeded to carve from the wild land around the cottage the meadows which became their flower farm.

Also by Derek Tangye in Sphere Books:

LAMA
SOMEWHERE A CAT IS WAITING
A DONKEY IN THE MEADOW
SUN ON THE LINTEL
WHEN THE WINDS BLOW
A CAT AFFAIR
THE WAY TO MINACK
THE WINDING LANE
COTTAGE ON A CLIFF
THE AMBROSE ROCK
A GULL ON THE ROOF
A DRAKE AT THE DOOR
A CORNISH SUMMER

A Cat in the Window

DEREK TANGYE

Sketches by Jean Tangye

SPHERE BOOKS LIMITED
London and Sydney

First published in Great Britain by Michael Joseph Ltd 1962
First published in paperback by New English Library Ltd 1972
Copyright © by Derek Tangye 1962
Published by Sphere Books Ltd 1984
30–32 Gray's Inn Road, London WC1X 8JL
Reprinted 1985

TRADE
MARK

Printed and bound in Great Britain by
Cox & Wyman Ltd, Reading

To Jeannie's mother

A Cat in the Window

1

THE opening paragraph of my book, *A Gull on the Roof*, which told how we came to live in Cornwall, was about our cat Monty of whom I said: 'He was, for both Jeannie and myself, the repository of our secret thoughts.' I am writing the story of Monty in *A Cat in the Window*.

I first met Monty in Room 205 of the Savoy Hotel. He was six weeks old, and when I came into the room was tumbling, chasing, biting, an old typewriter ribbon dragged temptingly across the carpet by Lois, Jeannie's secretary. He was the size and colour of a handful of crushed autumn bracken. At the time I did not notice the distinguishing marks I was later to know so well – the silky white shirt front, the smudge of orange on the left paw, the soft maize colour of the fur on his tummy. I did not notice his whiskers, nor his tail with its dark rings against cream, the rings graduating in size to the tip which, in his lifetime, was to flick this way and that, a thousand, thousand times. I saw only a pretty kitten with great big innocent eyes gambolling in the incongruous setting of Jeannie's office, and I wondered why.

'What's this?' I said to Lois, looking down at the two of them, 'what on earth is this kitten doing here?' I had seen Ambassadors, film stars, famous journalists, politicians of all parties, in Jeannie's office, but I had never before met a cat. It made me suspicious.

'Come on,' I said, 'come on, Lois, tell me what it's all about?' But Lois, the perfect secretary, went on playing as if she hadn't heard me. 'Lois, you're hiding something from me. Where's Jeannie? What's she been up to? Both of you know I dislike cats and if ...'

'She'll be back soon.' Lois was smiling and refusing to be drawn. 'She had to go over to Claridge's. General Montgomery has just arrived and nobody is allowed to know. She won't be long.' As Public Relations Officer of the Savoy Group it was part of Jeannie's job to keep certain news from the Press, just as much as it was on other occasions to get other news widely publicised.

But on this occasion, on this particular warm, summer afternoon as I awaited her return with Lois

10

and the chocolate box cover of a kitten, her task was specially important.

Monty had arrived to make a progress report to Churchill on the Battle of the Desert.

I came from a dog family. In the walled garden of my rambling Cornish home was a row of wooden crosses with painted cries of Victorian sentiment. 'Alas, poor Rosa,' 'Sweet, gentle Cara,' 'Farewell Little Gyp.' And in my own childhood I remember the crosses going up again. My parents had no desire to disclose their emotions so, in their day, only the birth and death and name of the dog appeared on the cross. Rex, Bulger, Bruce, Mary, Lance, Roy, Gay. These sparse tributes to devotion were sometimes countered in my mind by unexpectedly finding my father standing opposite a cross quietly puffing his pipe. Young as I was, it touched me to feel the memories that were passing through him.

My personal friends were first Bruce and then Lance; or Sir Lancelot by which, until I found the name too much of a mouthful, I first called him. Bruce was a mongrel of indescribable parentage while Lance, an Old English Sheepdog, brought with him from the kennels where he was born a list of relations bearing the names of sheepdog royalty. Bruce was in our family before I was born and by the time I was seven I thought he was immortal. He was to me a brother of my own age, and for hours on end I would tease him or wrestle or play hide and seek with him among the gorse and tamarisk covered land around our home. Bruce was the answer to any doubts of my mother as to how I could spend my time.

Then he died and grief being suddenly to me an emotion instead of a word, my father countered by producing Lance. He moved subtly. He knew that what I needed was a dog I could call my own, and he devised a means that would make me, the small boy, feel he was my own. He told me one evening after I had gone to bed that he was driving to London the following morning and that, if I liked, I could go with him to Exeter, then return to Newquay by myself on the Cornish Riviera. He made me feel grown up and, unsuspectingly, I excitedly accepted. But when we reached Exeter station and the Riviera rolled in I found I was not to be alone on my return journey; for in the guards van curled timidly in a wicker basket was Lance.

I matured with Lance. First the same childish games I had with Bruce, then the tearful partings before school terms, wild barking reunions, and soon the long walks of doubtful youth, Lance at my side in the winding lines sharing my puzzlement. I was a man when Lance died.

Dogs, then, had been entities in my life. Cats, as if they were wasps with four legs, had been there to shoo away. They did not belong in my life nor in my family's life. All of us were united that whenever we saw a cat the most important thing to do was to see it out of sight.

But as I moved slowly out of the environment of my family, I found naturally enough people and homes

12

who accepted cats as we accepted dogs. Cats were not vulgar, as, in some mysterious way, I had been led to believe. I began to note that cats were able to bestow a subtle accolade upon their apparent owners which made these owners rapturous with delight.

I resented this. Dogs, and by this I mean well mannered, full of character, devoted dogs who did not snarl or bark unnecessarily, were to me the true tenants of a home. Cats were vagrants. They did not merit affection.

I sensed, of course, that my attitude in a home where there was a cat or cats was unsatisfactory; so I developed a pose that after a while I made myself believe was genuine. I was allergic to cats. The proximity of one produced asthma. I felt dizzy. I behaved so strangely that any owner of a cat who was entertaining me was convinced that if I were not to prove a sickly embarrassment the cat had to be removed. I know there are some people who genuinely feel like this, but I was not one.

It was in this mood that I paid my first call on Jeannie's parents in their handsome house on the hill of St Albans. I sat down in the sitting-room and promptly Tim, Jeannie's cat, a huge blue Persian, jumped on my lap. Unthinkingly I played my customary part. I gave Tim a violent push and, in so doing, knocked over a small table upon which was my untouched cup of tea. From that moment I began to realise it was dangerous to appear to dislike cats.

For Jeannie is a cat lover, not only the slave of an individual, but an all-embracing cat lover. If she

sees a cat on the other side of the street she will want
to cross over to talk to it. Any pretty little thing, any
handsome Tom, will receive her caressing and cooing.
She fawns on the breed. Little wonder her mother
after my visit had ended cast a humorous doubt on a
successful marriage. Could a cat lover live happily
with a cat hater?

My future dealings with Tim were, therefore,
cautious. I was careful not to cause offence by throw-
ing any make-believe tantrums, yet I was equally
careful not to appear affected by the lofty gaze he
sometimes cast on me. I was polite but distant. I was
determined to hold fast to my traditional dislike of
the species. I was not going to be hypnotised by gentle
purs, soft kneading of paws, an elegant walk across
the room and a demand to jump on my knees. I
disliked cats. I most certainly would not have one in
our home after we had married.

This was my mood as I waited for Jeannie to return
from Claridge's. We had been married three months.

2

BUT I made no scene except a mock one. It was an inevitable defeat. I could only bluster. I could not enter my married life with an argument about a cat.

Monty chose the moment of Jeannie's return to pounce upon the toe of my shoe; then disappear up my trousers, except for a tail. He tickled my leg until I had to stoop and, for the first time, touch him. Jeannie and Lois watched hopefully the effect this would have on me. He was very soft, and the wriggle with which he tried to escape me was feeble, like the strength of my little finger. I felt the teeth nibble my hand, and a tiny claw trace a tickle on my skin; and when I picked him up and held him firmly in front of me, the big eyes stared childishly at me with impotent resentment. I had never held a cat in my hands before.

'This is diabolical,' I said in pretence fury, addressing Jeannie and Lois, 'and don't think I haven't a card up my sleeve . . . I'm going to chuck this thing over Hammersmith Bridge on the way home.' I spoke so vehemently that Lois seemed half to believe me. 'Yes I am,' I said, rubbing it in, 'I'll stop the car and fling the cat over the parapet.'

'Kitten,' murmured Lois.

'Monty,' said Jeannie.

There is no defence against women who sense your heart has already surrendered. The head, however astute in presenting its arguments, appears hollow. If Jeannie wanted Monty she had to have him. How could I deny her? The best I could do was to learn to tolerate his existence; and make an attempt to impose conditions.

'All right, I won't do *that*,' I said, and was immediately irked by the gleam of victory in their eyes, 'But I'll tell you what I *will* do . . . ' I looked defiantly at both of them. 'I'll make quite certain he is a *kitchen* cat. There'll be no question of him wandering about the house as if he owns it.'

This display of authority eased me into seeing the situation in a more comforting perspective. Jeannie would be happy, Monty out of sight, and I could continue my aloofness towards the species as before.

'But if he doesn't behave himself,' I added, looking

at the little ball of fur in my hand, 'he'll have to be found another home.'

The weakness in my attack was my responsibility for Monty's arrival. It was indirect, but a fact. We had mice in our cottage at Mortlake; and when, at Jeannie's request, I set traps and caught the mice, I was so sickened by the task of releasing the dead mouse from the trap that I preferred to throw both the mouse and the trap into the river.

The cottage, with a roof the shape of a dunce's cap, was within a few yards of the finishing post of the Boat Race, and only the towpath separated the front steps and the river. On the ground floor was the dining-room, the kitchen and the spare bedroom; on the first, two bedrooms, one overlooking the river, and the other the garden; and on the top floor were the bathroom and the sitting-room which stretched the breadth of the cottage. Across this room at door level stretched two massive old oak beams and from them, dove-tailed by wooden pegs, were two spans ancient as the beams, triangular, supporting the inside of the dunce's cap which was the ceiling. In one corner was the fireplace and op-osite, along the length of the room, were the windows from which we watched the Thames flowing to the curve at Barnes Bridge; and beyond, the silhouette of London.

The cottage was once upon a time an inn, and one of the innkeepers was a waterman who married a Shakespeare player. I used to dig up broken old clay pipes in the garden, sometimes part of a stem, sometimes a bowl, and when I sent a sample to the British Museum they confirmed they were Elizabethan. From then on I used to hand pieces to visitors, telling them the story of the cottage. 'You had better keep this,' I would say, 'Shakespeare may have used it.'

It was a small walled garden the length of a cricket pitch and the width of half a tennis court. At the top end was the concrete shelter in which we crouched during bad air raids . . . except the night we were celebrating our first wedding anniversary with a party in the cottage; and the roof was blown off.

On the other side of one wall was the garden of the Ship, the pub next door; on the other side of the opposite one was a passage-way from the river to Mortlake village; and within a hundred yards of both were Sandy Lane and West Road with the Brewery towering in the background. Along the river bank were three or four houses and beyond them, three minutes from the cottage, was Chiswick Bridge. In time, in the early morning, Monty used to walk with us to the Bridge but he would go no farther. He would sit down when we reached the archway and, however much we coaxed him, would not budge. He was never, in fact, to be a wanderer while he lived at Mortlake. His world, for seven years, was to be the small walled garden; except after the bombing when he came with us to Jeannie's old home at St Albans. And it was from St Albans in the first place that he came.

I complained once again one morning to Jeannie about my trap task. In retrospect I know, of course,

I was being ridiculous, but at the time, when I had to perform the task, I felt disgusted.

'Now if we had a cat,' replied Jeannie, and she gave no sign that she was trying to influence me unduly, 'you wouldn't have to worry about traps at all . . . you see, the very smell of a cat keeps mice away.'

In due course I was to find this statement to be untrue, but at the time, in the frame of mind I was in on that particular morning, it interested me.

'You mean to say that a mouse never comes into a house where there's a cat, and all that catching and squealing takes place outside?'

'Oh, yes,' said Jeannie blandly, 'mice are very intelligent and they know they haven't a chance if a cat finds them in a house.'

'And what about birds?' Jeannie, I knew, once had a favourite cat called Tubby who spent much of her time in the spring climbing up trees to catch nestlings for her kittens. Jeannie, when she could, would gently take the little bird from Tubby's mouth when she reached her kittens and return it to the nest.

'Well,' she said, making the answer sound very simple, 'all you have to do is to have the cat doctored. Cats only catch birds for their families.'

Here again the ardour to convert me misled her sense of accuracy. True, Monty was seen to catch only one bird in his life, and that was a wren which annoyed him and which he promptly let go when we advanced on him; but he, I think was an exception. Most cats, if they don't catch for their families, will catch for the fun of it, or because they are bored.

21

You can't blame them. They are no worse than the man who takes out his gun for an hour or two of rough shooting.

'Anyhow,' I said, by way of ending the conversation, 'I still don't like them.'

On reflection, I believe my dislike was based on their independence. A dog, any dog, will come to you wagging its tail with friendliness if you click your fingers or call to it. There is no armed neutrality between the dog world and the human race. If a human is in need of affection and there is a dog about, he is sure to receive it, however frail affection from a stranger may be. Dogs are prepared to love; cats, I believed were not.

I had observed too, that cat owners (but who, I wondered, would call himself the owner of a cat?) were apt to fall into two types. Either they ignored the cat, put it out at night whatever the weather, left it to fend for itself when they went away on holidays, and treated it, in fact, as a kind of better class vermin; or else they worshipped the animal like a god. The first category appeared callous, the second devoid of sense.

I had seen, for instance, a person sit rigid and uncomfortable in a chair because a cat had chosen his lap as the whim of its own particular comfort. I had noticed, and been vexed by her, the hostess who hastens away at the end of a meal with titbits for the cat which has stared balefully at her guests during the course of it. Cats, it seemed to me, aloofly hinted the power of hypnotism; and as if in an attempt to

ward off this uncanniness, their owners pandered to
them, anxiously trying to win approval for themselves
by flattery, obedience, and a curious vocabulary of
nonsensical phrases and noises. A cat lover, I had
found, was at the mercy of the cat.

I was now to learn for myself whether this was true.
My education was about to begin. My morning
conversation with Jeannie had made her believe
there might be a gap in my armour; and by the time
I had forgotten the conversation, she had already
rung up her mother to disclose her hopes. 'I think he's
weakening,' she said, 'We must seize the chance.'

And so no time was lost. Her mother had an
appointment at the hairdressers and she promised
that immediately afterwards she would go to the
pet shop to see what kittens were available. The
visit never took place. At the hairdressers she con-
fided her mission to the girl who attended her. 'But
I've got a kitten that nobody wants,' the girl said,
'it's a ginger, the last of a litter, and if we don't find
a home by tomorrow he'll have to be put away.'

I would not have agreed if my advice had been
sought. One less kitten in the world would not have
seemed very important to me. But my advice wasn't
sought and Monty was saved.

For the price of my mother-in-law's weekly
chocolate ration, he entered our lives.

3

As soon as I picked him out of the wicker basket in which we had brought him home, I explained to our housekeeper that Monty was to be a kitchen cat. 'I don't want to see him at all,' I said, 'he's here to catch mice and although he may be small for that yet, I've been told the very smell of a cat will keep them away.'

I looked at Jeannie. She was busily unwrapping a small paper parcel. 'Isn't that true? Didn't you say that?'

'Oh yes . . . yes.'

An object had now appeared from the paper. A small *sole bonne femme*. It was freshly cooked and succulent.

'Good heavens, Jeannie,' I said, 'where did you get that?'

'Latry gave it to me,' she said. Latry was the famous maître chef of the Savoy. 'He's cooked it specially as a celebration present for Monty.' I looked at the fish and then at Monty. Only a few hours before, the girl in the hairdressers was frightened he would be put away on the morrow.

'Really, Jeannie,' I said crossly, 'you can't go cadging food for the cat.'

'I wasn't cadging. Latry *gave* it to me, I tell you. He loves cats and felt honoured to cook Monty's first meal.'

'Honoured,' I murmured to myself, and shuddered.

Jeanie mashed the fish up in a saucer, put it on the floor and began cooing at Monty who, never having seen a fish before, tottered off in the opposite direction.

'There you are,' I said, as if I had achieved a minor triumph, 'he doesn't like fish.'

Of course he was soon to do so; and during the course of his life he was to eat vast quantities of it, although sole was not his favourite. It was whiting. The cottage, and also in due course our cottage in Cornwall, was often to reek with the stink of it when the water in which it was cooked boiled over from the pan on to the stove.

But on the first morning of his life with us, the

morning on which I awoke to a disquieting awareness
that the pattern of my life was about to be re-adjusted,
the sole from the Savoy kitchens awaited him. 'I
wonder whether he has eaten it,' pondered Jeannie
aloud as she dressed.

Oddly enough I found myself wondering too. It
was as if time being momentarily dull I was awaiting
the BBC News to hear if the announcer had anything
to say to stir the pulse. 'I'll go down and see,' I said,
and was off through the door in my dressing gown.

The stairs were narrow and steep, of polished wood
and slippery; and on the third step from the bottom,
too frightened to go up or down, was Monty. 'How
have you got there?' I said; and my voice was as
firm as could be allowed when a child gets caught in a
predicament. 'Your place is in the kitchen. It's no
use you trying to learn to climb stairs.' The tiny
miaows did not protest against my firmness, they
appealed for my help; and so I picked him up in
one hand and took him to the saucer of the night
before where it had been placed under the kitchen
table. It was empty.

Jeannie was encouraged by my apparent gentleness
on this occasion; and I observed, during the days
that followed, how she cunningly began to use Monty
to help pierce my utilitarian attitude towards him.
The process continued from days into weeks until
one afternoon an incident took place which, she
considered, set the seal on her triumphant tactics.

The first of these tactics was her good sense in
realising it was unwise to make too much fuss of

Monty in my presence. She made up for this apparent coolness in my absence, but this I was not to know; and I was not to know, for instance, that Latry, the Chef, continued to supply her with delicacies which she fed to Monty surreptitiously while I was in the pub next door.

Nor when, as he grew older, he began successfully to climb the stairs, did she encourage him to do so; and on the evening he was found for the first time in a tight ball on the bed, she impressed me with her scolding. Indeed I felt a twinge of sympathy for Monty as I carried him, on Jeannie's instructions, back to the kitchen. I found myself wondering against my will whether it was fair he should be banished when it was so obvious he was prepared to give both of us his affection.

Monty played his own part very well because from the beginning he made it plain he liked me. It was a dangerous moment of flattery when I realised this and I believe, had it not been for my entrenched posture of dislike for the species, I would have fallen for it without more ado. There was, however, a thick enough layer of prejudice inside me for me to hold out.

He would seek to play with me. I would be sitting at dinner and feel a soft cushion gently knocking my foot, and when I put down a hand to stop it my fingers were enclosed by small teeth. In the garden he would perform his most bewitching tricks in front of me, the clumsy chase of a butterfly, the pounce on an imaginary demon leaving a spreadeagled posterior to face me. And when at the end of the day we returned to the cottage, unlatched the door and went inside, it was strange how often he came to me instead of paying court to Jeannie. Did I perhaps impose an intuition upon him that my prejudice, once defeated, would leave a vacuum that he alone could fill? My prejudice has long ago disappeared, but I am still a one cat man. I have never developed a taste for a household of cats, each with a colourful name, each having to share the affection accorded to them all, each leading a life so independent that one of them can disappear for a few days without causing undue worry. It is a taste in cat worship I will never share. I am incapable of spreading my affection so widely. Monty needed only to vanish for a few hours and we both would fill ourselves with imaginary fears.

But the talk of these cat lovers among Jeannie's friends was part of my education. She enlisted their aid. I listened to the language they used, both spoken and unspoken, and became aware there was a streak of connoisseurship in this world of cats. It was the snobbery of an exclusive club; and if the flavour of conversation was an acquired taste, it was no more so than learning to like jazz or Bach. They perused Monty and unanimously pronounced he would grow into a beautiful member of the fraternity; and fraternity henceforth replaced for me the words of species or breed. They admired his head and foretold, quite correctly, it would become like that of a miniature tiger, not snouty and elongated like some ginger cats. They assessed his mother as a tortoiseshell and his father as a tabby. They liked his whiskers which at that age were wisps of white. They forecast, as he had been doctored, that he would become a huge cat. They discussed him, men and women of distinction in various walks of life, in the tone one associates with relations probing the future of an infant of noble heritage. Would his appearance measure up to his responsibilities? Young as he was, did he show signs of a strong character? Would his movements prove elegant? How thick would become his coat? Monty was fussed over and cooed at as if to win his favour was an ambition far out-weighing in importance any achievement in the daily task. I watched amused, comforting myself with the knowledge that Jeannie's friends were not as serious as they appeared. Monty was only a diversion. He was a toy for temporary enjoyment. A cat could never possess a personality which could be remembered except by those with whom he lived.

In any case, during the initial period of this homage bestowed on him, Monty did not appear very attractive. He would not wash. His body was dull and dusty, the white on his left paw a dirty cuff, the crescent of white on his little chest a grey, soiled shirt. 'He looks like an alley cat,' I taunted Jeannie.

My coolness towards him, my inclination to niggle at any of his failings, naturally increased the sense of protection she had for him; and during this phase of unwash she was afraid I might have the excuse to get rid of him. Yet, to my surprise, I did not feel that way at all. I too, felt a sense of protection; and the evening, Jeannie have gone home before me, I returned to find Monty on a chair in the kitchen his fur shining bright, I was as delighted as Jeannie. I did not know she had damped him all over with plain water; and he had licked himself dry.

It was another homecoming a few weeks later, an unexpected one, which finally witnessed my capitulation. I had spent the day in the cottage and was not thinking of Jeannie's return till the evening. I was in the top room alone when there was a noise at the door as if it were being kicked by a soft boot. I opened it and Monty came scampering in. He rushed to the sofa, jumped up, climbed on the back walking along it tail up, then down again to the floor and across to where I was standing, arching his back, rubbing his head against my leg and purring. All this in less than a minute, and performed with such élan that it made me wonder whether he was telling me in his particular fashion that I had been making an ass of myself. I bent down and stroked him, and he thereupon carried out a manoeuvre which he was often to do when he aimed to be especially endearing. He twisted his head as if he were going to fold up in a ball, collapsed on the floor and turned over, and lay with his back on the green carpet, paws in the air, displaying his silky maize underparts while a pair of bright yellow eyes hopefully awaited the pleasure the sight would give me. The reward he expected was a gentle stroke until he decided he had had one too many when there would be a savage mock attempt to bite my fingers.

But on this first occasion I was holding a pipe

cleaner in my hand and I tickled him with that, which led to a game, which led half an hour later to his sitting on my desk, a large kidney shaped Regency desk with a top like a table, performing ridiculous antics with a pencil.

I was sitting there roaring with laughter when the door opened. In walked Jeannie.

4

My capitulation was complete, and within a few weeks there was no pretence that Monty was a kitchen cat. Every room in the cottage was his kingdom; and at night, if his fancy was to sleep on the bed, I would lie with legs stiff so as not to disturb him while he curled in a ball at the bottom. I endlessly wanted to play with him, and felt put in my place when he was not in the mood, stalking away from me tail in the air showing he had something more important to do, like a vigorous if temporary wash of the underparts.

Sometimes my games were gently malicious, as if

taking a friendly revenge on the way he had captured me. I used to lift him on to the beam in the sitting-room where he glared down at me, then ran along the beam to find a place from which to leap on to the floor, only to find I had moved along too and was there to stop him. I would put up a hand and receive a slap from a paw.

There was another game with an ulterior purpose or game perhaps is the wrong word for it. Three months had gone by and there was still no evidence that he had caught a mouse; no remains had been found, no victory bellow heard, no sign that there were fewer mice than before. It was disturbing. His presence had brought no fear to the mice and so he seemed as useless as a dog for the purpose required of him. 'Perhaps he left his mother too soon,' said Jeannie, apologising, 'and she didn't have time to teach him.'

I no longer wished to prise Jeannie's defences and whereas in the beginning I would have ridiculed such a remark, I now said nothing. Monty was growing fast and his appetite enormous, so the best thing to do, I decided, was to keep him hungry for a while and let his natural cat's instinct develop out of necessity. After twenty-four hours he was prowling around like a tiger, and Jeannie was yearning to yield to his fury. 'You're cruel,' she said, 'to do this to him.' It was often to be like that, Jeannie always ready to surrender to his whims while I, my anti-cat upbringing still somewhere within me, endeavoured to insist on discipline.

But my plan on this occasion was to put him up in the attic, a dark, forbidding world of rafters, cobwebs and, without doubt, mice. Standing on a chair, my arms outstretched above me, I shoved Monty through the trap door, and returned to the sitting-room to await results. After half an hour Jeannie argued it was time to let him out. After an hour I was restraining her from standing on the chair. She was furious. I was anxious less my plan had misfired. Another ten minutes and I admitted I was wrong. I stood on the chair to push upwards the trap door. At that instant there was a wild scramble on the ceiling, followed by squeak, squeak, squeak . . and a few seconds later peering down from the opening above me was Monty with a mouse like a fat moustache, in his mouth.

As Monty grew larger Jeannie's lap became too small for his comfort, and he transferred to mine. He would approach where I was sitting, arch his back, claw for a brief second at the chair's fabric, leap up and settle down, then turn his head upward to me as if he were saying: 'Thank you very much.' That was not, however, the moment when I required any thanks because I always felt flattered he had chosen me, above all other comfortable spots in the house, to rest on a while. It was later when I deserved the thanks, when my feet had gone to sleep, my legs had got cramp, and I had refrained from doing any job I had intended to do. I never dared move him. I would watch him comfortably dozing, occasionally adjusting his posture while I sat stiff as a ramrod: such a gesture as selecting my lap was an accolade I could not refuse. I was to spend hours, days, weeks of my life like that, while Jeannie sat opposite watching the two of us.

There were times, however, when first he paid me this attention, that circumstances forced me to move him. It was the period of the little blitz, the bitter late winter when Hitler again attacked London. The sirens would wail while we sat upstairs in the sitting room and we would wait, pretending we were not tense, until the guns began firing. 'They're not very busy tonight,' I would sometimes say, which only meant I had not heard any bombs fall in the neighbourhood. But there were other times when a stick would fall uncomfortably close, and then I would tuck Monty under my arm and we would all hasten to the shelter at the top of the garden. We would crouch there, the dark being flashed into brilliance while Jeannie, a hand clutching Monty, would declare she was more afraid of the spiders than she was of the bombs.

On the night a near miss blew the roof off, leaving our sitting-room facing the stars, we were not in the shelter. It was the evening of our first wedding anniversary and a number of friends were celebrating with us when we heard the stick coming . . . one, two, three, four and wham! The Brewery had a direct hit and the fire that followed lit the night into daylight, and we knew that this tempting sight might lead to another attack. None of us was hurt, only covered with plaster, but the room we loved so much was a terrible sight; and Jeannie and I were standing

at the door looking at it, thinking how only an hour
or two before we had spent such care getting it
ready when suddenly she said: 'Where's Monty?'

We ran down the stairs asking as we went whether
anyone had seen him. We ran into the kitchen shouting his name, then into the dining-room, then into
the spare bedroom that led from the kitchen. No one
had seen him. I ran into the garden calling his name,
the guns still firing, the flames in the Brewery leaping
into the sky; and I remember how even in that
moment of distress I found myself marvelling at the
silhouette of a fireman's ladder that was already
poised high against the fire, a pin-point of a man at
the top of it. 'Monty,' I yelled, 'Monty!' No sign of
him there so I went back to the house asking everyone
to look, then out on to the river bank where I knew
Jeannie had gone. I found her, but no Monty; and
after searching for a while we felt our task hopeless,
nothing to do except go home and wait. 'He'll turn
up,' I said, trying to encourage her.

And half an hour later into the kitchen came one
of our guests, a burly Australian war correspondent,
with Monty held in his arms like a child. His fur was
powdered with plaster, as white as if he had spent
the night in a bakery house.

'He'd got in his foxhole,' the Australian said with
a grin on his face, using the phrase of a soldier. 'I
found him upstairs in the airing cupboard!'

He was unharmed except for the temporary mess of
his fur; and later, when dawn was breaking and the
raiders had gone, he decided to sit on the kitchen

table and receive the homage of the firemen for whom Jeannie was pouring cups of tea. The powdery plaster had been licked away; and he sat, tail gently flicking, eyes blinking, dozing like a miniature tiger in the midday sun, utterly sure of himself amidst the hubbub of chatter. He was calmer than any of the humans around him.

And when, to commemorate this end of our first year of marriage, we asked the firemen to sign their names in the visitors' book, one of them scrawled alongside his signature:

'Monty, the handsomest cat I ever saw.'

5

WE left Mortlake two days later to become evacuees
with Jeannie's father and mother at St Albans; and
within an hour of arrival at his temporary home
there was an incident which had an effect on Monty
for the rest of his life. He had always been suspicious
of dogs, but until St Albans, he had never come face
to face with one in the same room.

Bryher Lodge stood on the hill facing east towards
London; and on nights when duties did not perforce
make us stay in the city we would stand on the terrace
above the garden which sloped down to the wood

43

at the bottom, and watch the inferno in the distance. First the little blitz, then, a few weeks later and shortly before we returned to the cottage, the beginning of the flying bombs. We would watch for a few minutes this insanity of the human race, then return indoors to the private war between Judy the Scottie in the house, and Monty.

With Judy, when we came, was Tim the Persian. Tim was the placid old cat with blue grey fur so thick that it made him look as if he was wearing a muff, whose unwelcome attention on my first visit resulted in me knocking over the table on which stood my cup of tea. I was friends with him now, of course, and he was so placid that even Monty's sudden appearance could not annoy him. Tim and Monty tolerated each other from the beginning but Judy, after one look at the evacuee, decided she would not give him a moment's peace. Monty was an interloper, and Judy was never to allow him to forget it.

My own opinion is that Jeannie and her mother were partly to blame because of the method of introduction they chose to arrange. I myself favoured a gradual acclimatisation, an interchange of leftover sniffs after one or the other had left the room, a sight of each other in the garden with one of them safely behind a window. I was cautious, I had an instinct of inevitable trouble if suddenly they were placed nose to nose.

I expect trouble was inevitable in any case, but it certainly exploded with the least delay. I unloaded our luggage, lumbered it up to the bedroom and then heard Jeannie cry out: 'Come on downstairs, we're going to introduce Monty to Judy.' Their theory, and I suppose there was some sense in it, was that as Judy and Monty were going to live in the closest proximity, they might as well learn to be friends as quickly as possible; and I arrived in the room just as the introduction was made.

It was over within thirty seconds. Judy leapt at Monty and snapped at his paw. Monty then jumped on a table crashing a vase, remained there for an instant with fur like an upturned brush, then on to the floor dashing between the legs of Jeannie's mother who grabbed him, holding him until he freed himself, whereupon he raced across to the blue velvet curtains, up them like a monkey and remained on the pelmet, snarling like a mad thing at Judy yapping hysterically below.

We ourselves, for a moment, were quite silent. Each of us was thinking how such enmity could possibly be handled during the weeks to come. Jeannie and I, and Monty, despite it being her old home were guests in the house and we could not be expected to be popular if we brought chaos along with us; and Jeannie's mother was saying to herself that at all costs the welcome of our arrival must be brought back to normal. She did so by never disclosing that Monty had gashed her so sharply with his claws that the following day she had four stitches in her arm.

Monty and Judy never came face to face again, yet the atmosphere of their hate remained. If one was allowed free in the house, the other was shut in a room; and the one which was free would be aware of the door behind which was the other. Judy would scratch, Monty would sniff and his fur rise up. It was an unhappy period for both of them, and the immediate effect on Monty was to lessen the affection he had for Jeannie and me. He became remote from us. There were no purrs. It was as if he had lost his personality and was just an animal on four legs which had no thought in its head except to eat and sleep. He would not play. He would not sleep on the bed. His behaviour, in fact, made me lose interest in him. He was a silly, characterless cat.

This zombie attitude continued for four months until, the cottage repaired, we returned home; and within a few minutes of our arrival Monty's old self returned too. He proved it by jumping out of the kitchen window. The window had been his own private entrance, not the main casement window but the small one above it, open and shut by a lever. We had always kept it half open for him, day and night, and he would leap to its frame, pause a moment and disappear outside; or at night we would be in the kitchen and become suddenly aware that Monty had silently appeared from the darkness without and was poised up there, watching us. On this occasion he had not been in the kitchen a minute before he jumped up to this window, then down to the garden; and without waiting he was up again to the window and into the kitchen. We watched him repeat this act, as if it were a celebration dance, four or five times; and as we watched we could sense the dull attitude which had developed disappearing, and the old relationship becoming real again. 'He's actually glad to be home,' I said to Jeannie, as if I were surprised such a feeling could exist within him. 'He really *knows* he's home.'

My simplicity had its reaction later that night when I was lying awake. I found myself thinking that as I had learnt to get on perfectly well without considering Monty while at St Albans, I had better do the same now at home. I was retracing my steps. I was having a midnight revolt against my over indulgence of the cat. I had been hastening to become as cooing as the cat lovers I used to despise, submerging my own personality for Monty's benefit, becoming a slave to his wayward habits; and it was time for me to stop.

St Albans had taught me that one could give a roof to a cat without losing one's own identity; and although Monty had been plainly uncomfortable he did not run away, he remained clean, he had a good appetite. He could, therefore, lead a useful but negative life with us at the cottage, have his meals and his freedom to wander about, but, as at St Albans, there was no need for him to enter the stream of our life.

I would not, for instance, become excited just because he jumped in and out of the kitchen window. I would not consider myself favoured when he sat on my lap; I would push him off it it suited me. Lying there in the dark I realised I had been showing all the faults of the convert, all the undisciplined enthusiasm the novice displays. I had been behaving, before the change at St Albans, like a fawning servant before its master. It was ridiculous and tomorrow I must set out to regain my independence whatever tricks Monty might produce. Of course Jeannie was going to be difficult; but if I were cunning, if I did not take any positive action against Monty, if I were polite but distant, she would have no need to suspect the great change that had suddenly taken place inside me.

She was sound asleep, and Monty was also on the bed, down at the bottom alongside my feet. I suddenly thought: why not set the pace of my new attitude towards him immediately? My legs were cramped and had he not been occupying so much room, I could have stretched them and been comfortable, and I might even have fallen asleep. Here goes, I said to myself; and gave him a shove. A second later there was a thud on the floor, then, a few seconds later he was on the bed again. Another shove. Another thud.

And at that moment Jeannie woke up, shouting excitedly as one does when alarmed from a dream: 'What's wrong? What's wrong?'

'Nothing at all,' I said soothingly, 'only Monty fell off.'

6

MONTY'S memory of Judy, had he been human, might have been eradicated on a psychiatrist's couch; but as it was the rage he felt against her simmered inside him, erupting in an explosion at intervals during the rest of his life. He was determined to fight a ceaseless battle of revenge.

His first victory, soon after our return, was over a bulldog pup belonging to a friend who lived close by. Outside our front door was a tiny garden, enclosed by a three foot wall to help keep out the high tides of the Thames; and we went over this wall from the garden to the tow path by a ladder of stone steps.

These steps were never a particular favourite of Monty's, indeed he usually avoided the tiny front garden as if he disliked the bustle of the towpath on the other side of the wall; but on occasions he liked to sun himself there, and one pleasant morning he was lying on the top step when along came the bull-dog pup.

The pup was a bandy-legged brindle and he came jauntily down the alleyway from his home with a sniff here and a sniff there, up to the pillarbox and across to the lamp-post. I was standing myself by the open front door and I watched him amusedly; he looked like a school-boy on holiday without a care in the world.

But Monty was watching as well. He watched until the pup was within five yards of the steps, then crouching as if to spring at a mouse, he waited for it to come another yard nearer . . . and pounced. I was so surprised that I just stared; but the pup, thank goodness, had been attracted the same instant by the railings on the other side of the towpath; and he moved away as Monty sprang, so his stumpy stern met the onslaught instead of his back. A yell of fright from the pup and it set off at a gallop for Chiswick Bridge. It was still galloping long after Monty had stopped the chase; for Monty, as if to put fear into a bulldog was victory enough, returned nonchalantly to the steps after a chase of a few yards and unconcernedly began an elaborate wash. He never attacked the pup again, it never came near enough to let him.

Monty did not seek out his battles with dogs, creating a quarrel because he had nothing else to do. I often, for instance, saw him sitting in contemplation while a dog passed by without his ever making a move. It was when we were about that he became enraged. He either considered himself our protector or, more likely, the memory of Judy ground such jealousy in his mind that for a few moments he reverted to the wild cat of the jungle. No dog was safe whatever the size or breed and, for that matter, no human was safe who tried to stop the attack.

The first human to suffer was an elderly lady who arrived at the cottage with a small terrier on a lead. We did not fully appreciate Monty's temper at the time, and we had taken no steps to shut him in a room when the lady and the terrier entered the downstairs hall. Bang! Monty was hurtling out of the kitchen straight at the terrier and in the shambles that followed the poor lady was gashed in the leg. I had to take her to hospital.

This incident, of course, put us on our guard. We had so to speak to put a notice outside the front door: 'Beware of the Cat.' We had to meet anyone who arrived with a dog and shout: 'Wait out there a minute while we put Monty away.' And if Monty could not be found, the visitor and the dog had to be sneaked in, then rushed upstairs to the sitting-room, and the door firmly shut. Then, when the visit was over, I would act as a scout and see whether Monty was lurking anywhere on the stairs. I had to act like a conspirator, and I used to be thankful when the visitor and his dog were safely waved away.

Yet I never met a dog owner who did not at first believe we were playing a joke. Dog owners inflict their doggy devotion on others more officiously than their cat counterparts, or some of them do. Some dog owners I have found, for instance, are either deaf or peculiarly insensitive. They shut a dog in a house or shed in the garden, and have a sadistic relish in the barks that follow for hour after hour, bringing despair and wild exasperation to the neighbours. It is a form of torture to which I am particularly vulnerable. I lie awake at night and each bark is a hammer blow, and if it comes from a distance, from somewhere unknown to me, I have an uncontrollable desire to get dressed and go searching for the exact source of the hell. The daytime yap, the yap, yap, yap on some afternoon in high summer has seen me seize a stick and march towards the noise, only to halt a few minutes later and go back. For what is the use of action? It is a strange thing about such dog owners, if you complain, if you say you cannot sleep, or get on with your work, or that you are being driven slowly mad, you are seldom met with apologies. You are made to feel it is your fault, certainly not that of the dog or its owner.

Cats, of course, make a hullabaloo on the tiles but only if other cats are there too. Cats on their own are silent while a dog on its own will still bark. Cats may impose their personalities on visitors to their homes but, as they are too independent to go on visits themselves, strange homes are spared them.

Dogs bounce out of the car on arrival, go galloping over the flower beds in excitement, ignoring the cries of discipline; or come on a rainy day, shaking their wet coats, mapping the carpet with muddy paws. In our case, however, we had Monty; and so whenever a dog appeared one of us would cry out the alarm: 'Look out, Monty's about!'

The snag lay in the fact that unless the dog owner had visited us before, the reaction was not what we intended. The answer to our alarm was a display of supreme confidence.

'Oh don't worry,' would come the lofty reply, 'Our dog *never* chases cats!' We would try to explain how it would be Monty who did the chasing. 'Don't you understand?' we pleaded, 'Monty will chase *your* dog!' Meanwhile the dog would be running around and, in the distance, we would see a menacing Monty approaching.

At Mortlake we had the front door as the barrier, and so a clash was comparatively easy to avert. But when we came to live at remote Minack, our cottage in Cornwall, Monty could be lying in wait anywhere. Hence the attacks at Minack were more frequent. Monty was only making certain he would never again share his life with a dog.

It was also at the time of his return from St Albans that he developed a growl. Most cats growl at some time or other but it is a sound that is a close cousin to a purr. Monty's growl was a deep throated challenge of such resonance that he might have acquired it from one of the larger dogs he hated. Yet it was not a weapon of war, a threat to frighten an opponent.

It was a means of self reassurance, a method of bolstering himself when he found himself in a situation not to his liking. Any odd noise he did not understand would bring forth the growl and, for that matter, any big noise too. He growled at the guns which fired at the flying bombs, and at thunder, and when rockets took the place of flying bombs he growled at them. The first rocket which ever landed in Britain landed within a mile of Mortlake; and it is Monty's growl I remember, not the explosion.

Sometimes the growl made us laugh because he uttered it when caught in a predicament. There was an elm tree close to the cottage at Mortlake and up it he went one day, leaping from branch to branch, higher and higher, showing no sign he was soon to lose his nerve. I have never understood this particular blind spot of cats, how time and again they will climb to inaccessible places with the greatest of ease, then become transfixed by the height they have reached. I hate heights myself. I have an occasional nightmare which has me racing to the top of Everest; nothing hinders my climb, no hint of fear, until there I am looking out above the world . . . and quite incapable of descending. Monty too was incapable of descending and I had to fetch a ladder, and when the ladder did not reach him I had to climb up to him branch by branch. He was obviously terrified but he was not miaowing. He was growling.

A time came when we had chickens at the top of the garden, a dozen Rhode Island Reds penned in a small compound by wire netting on the side that faced the garden. On the other sides were high walls and on some point on these walls Monty would sit looking down on them while they clucked in troubled excitement. He was fascinated by their antics. Hour after hour he would crouch like a Buddha, eyeing them, trying to make up his mind what could be the purpose of their presence. At last he decided to make a closer investigation and he descended from the wall to the compound. I did not see him make his descent but I was in the garden reading a book when I heard the cacophony that hens make when a fox is among them. It was only Monty, an embarrassed Monty, surrounded by twelve furious ladies whom he was keeping at bay with his growl.

7

My midnight revolt, my show of independence when I kicked Monty off the bed, was in retreat by next morning. It takes two to sustain a revolt. You cannot keep up a revolt if the opposition insists on showing affection. Monty ignored my off-hand behaviour, forcing himself on my lap whenever he wished to do so, kneading my knees with his claws, letting me watch his back bulge like bellows with his purrs. For my part I could not refrain from stroking his silky fur, gently massaging his backbone and tracing a finger round his beautiful markings. I would have

59

been of stone if I hadn't. His presence was therapeutic, and he brought a calm to the hectic life we led.

In the years which followed the end of the war we were seldom home in the evenings except at week-ends. The nature of our work rushed us from party to party and we used to return home increasingly exhausted as the week developed. One becomes casual in such circumstances. One is so absorbed in fulfilling the basic responsibilities, that one is inclined to be blind to the subtleties that enrich life. Monty was a subtlety, and although we were always sure to give him a rapturous greeting whatever hour of the night we got back, he was, I think, treated by us more as a toy than an animal. It was a period that I look back upon as distressing; and yet it had its value. It helped us in due course to form our decision to pack up our jobs and leave London. It helped us, for instance, to realise it is more important to be true to oneself than to accept unthinkingly the standards of others.

Monty, in this period, was like a toy because the haste in our life only spared us the time to bestow affection on our own terms. He was like a child in a Victorian family who was shoved into the drawing-room by a nurse only at times when the parents were in a mood to see him. He would be used as a recep-tacle of our emotions, hugged and kissed in times of distress, expected to play games if we demanded them, shown off like an exhibit to appropriate friends. I have seen many cats, and dogs, treated in this way, and have disliked the sight of it. When human beings use their pet animals as agents of their own exhibitionism it means humiliation both for the human being and the animal; except that the human being concerned is too dumb to feel it. Often, of course, there are people who are frightened to show affection, or think it a curious kind of bad form either in themselves or in others; hence they consider pets should be treated as if behind bars in a zoo. These are the people who bury a cat or a dog one day, and buy a substitute the next, preferably of the same colour or breed so that the sequence of outward appearance remains undisturbed. Sometimes, of course, this is done not because of callousness but of fear, a fear of being unable to live a while with a memory. Either case provides an attitude which is unfair to the pet; for the first suggests it was no more important than an old kitchen chair while the second proposes that the death of a friendship can be swopped for a physical resemblance. I do not advocate a mourning, but I suggest that as a pet is a giver during its life and a human is usually a taker, a human should not accept an animal in his home unless he is prepared to make sacrifices which deserve affection.

One can also go to the other extreme and behave to an animal like a neurosis-ridden parent to his child; who must not swim because the sea might be dangerous, or own a bicycle, or stay out after dark, or who is fussed over like an invalid. Pampered animals can be observed any day of the week. Yet this other extreme need not be a form of neurosis or, for that matter, of exhibitionism. One can love an animal overmuch because of its vulnerability, because it makes one feel secure in an insecure world, because as it grows older it reflects the years of one's life. In due course we loved Monty overmuch but at this time, at this brittle period of our life, he was a toy; which had the merits of an anchor in our restless existence.

He would glare at us from inside the dining-room window as we arrived home, the sweep of the headlights shining on his fierce face. 'We're in trouble again,' I would say as I put the key in the door. It was perfectly true that he had the knack of making us feel we had misbehaved, that two o'clock in the morning was a disgraceful hour to return home. We would switch on the light and hurry into the dining-room ready to gush a greeting, only to find he had not moved, that he was still staring out of the window pretending to be unaware of our arrival except for the sharp flicks of his tail.

Jeannie used to come ready to bribe on these occasions and after she had purposely clattered plates in the kitchen and unwrapped some small paper parcel that had been donated by the Savoy restaurant, Monty would enter with the air of a cat who was ready to let bygones be bygones. He would devour the delicacy, lick the pattern off the plate but, unfortunately, would not pay the price expected of him. Jeannie's caresses were spurned and he would struggle free from her arms, jump first on the sink then up through his private entrance above the kitchen window, and disappear into the night. He was an opportunist, not a weak character open to a bribe.

There were other times when there was no doubt he had become unhappy in our absence. I knew the sign when we stood at the front door and heard him come thumping down the bare wood stairs, wakened by the sound of the car as we drew up. 'He's only hungry,' I would say to Jeannie, mocking his greeting. But if he was hungry it was not the hunger which was the result of a bribe. He did not bellicosely clean the plate, then away into the night. He would eat a little then look up at us watching him; and I defy the person who does not believe he was saying thank you. And afterwards he would not refuse to pay the price of his meal. Jeannie was permitted to hug him. as many hugs as she wanted, and carry him upstairs and deposit him on the bed where he lay curled through the night. There was now no fear of my kicking him off.

He was not on his own all the time. We did not leave him at nine in the morning and let him fend for himself until our return at any old hour. He had his friends. There was our daily, Mrs Hales, who had to queue for his whiting before she arrived at the cottage; whiting the staple diet, with the stink that hung for hours in the cottage. Mrs Hales was ill one day but as she lay in her bed she realised that the whiting, bought and cooked two days before, must have been consumed. 'Oh dear,' she said, explaining the situation to us later, 'oh dear, there I lay thinking of poor Monty. Whatever will he do, I said. All by 'imself and nothing to eat. It mustn't be I said. So I got up and called a neighbour through the window. 'Our Monty,' I said, ''asn't got 'is whiting. Do me a favour will you?' I said, 'go to the fish shop and get three nice whiting. I can manage to cook 'em . . then I'll send me 'usband up to Monty when 'e comes 'ome from work." '

There were Mr and Mrs Foster who lived next door at the Ship. The Fosters had been landlords since 1912, through the times when the Ship, as the pub at the finishing post of the Boat Race, was a pivot of the great day. Maharahahs, Cabinet Ministers, famous actors and actresses, as Gus and Olivette Foster never ceased telling us, used to be their customers then, shouting the crews to victory between glasses of champagne. There was none of that now; the bars were crowded on the big day, the steps of the pub and the towpath in front were jammed with people, but for the Fosters it was a poor imitation of what they remembered.

A high wall divided our small garden from theirs; and theirs was large enough for Gus Foster, in the distant past, to tether the trotting ponies the racing of which was once his hobby. This wall was Monty's favourite and he would reach it by way of the kitchen window and the flat roof of our spare room which ran along a short way beside it. Thus Monty, as he patrolled the top of this wall, could be observed not only from our side but also from the back windows of the Ship by anyone, such as the Fosters' son with the nickname of Whiskers, who might be at work in the garden.

Both Whiskers and his sister Doris had a particular interest in Monty, but as Doris worked in London during the day, it was Whiskers, the barman in the pub, who mostly kept a watch on his outside activities. He was in his garden one day digging a patch of ground when he heard a terrific hullabaloo on the other side of the wall as if it came through an open window from inside the house. Quite obviously the noise was of two fighting cats and one of them, presumably, was Monty.

Now the Fosters kept the key of our front door for just this kind of emergency, and Whiskers we always considered as a guardian of Monty in our absence. He was about to rush in for the key when the noise suddenly rose to a crescendo, followed a few seconds later by a huge tabby racing along the top of the wall with Monty at his tail. Whiskers said afterwards he was so delighted to see such a victory that he shouted: 'Well done, Monty!' at the top of his voice. But Monty, left alone on the wall after the tabby had fled over another, was obviously hurt. He lifted up a paw, looked down at Whiskers and miaowed loudly.

So Whiskers fetched the key and went inside our cottage and into the garden, and coaxed Monty down from the wall and into his arms. It was a nasty bite and we had the vet for him that evening; for Whiskers had immediately rung up Jeannie to tell her of the battle.

And what was the battle about? Instead of the stink of fish in the kitchen there was the stink of a tom cat. The tabby had stolen the whiting.

8

NOT only the Fosters but others along the river bank kept a watch on Monty. He was a talisman to the passers-by as he sat in the dining-room window, hour after hour, waiting for our return. One autumn we spent a month in Paris and when we got back we were looked at reproachfully by those who had seen him day after day in the window. 'You should have seen him late at night when the street lamp lit up his face,' said a neighbour, 'he looked so mournful.' We hated to hear such remarks because we felt we were in the wrong. Of course he had been well looked after by his guardians but he had been very lonely. And yet what does one do if ever one wishes to go away for a holiday with an easy conscience? Deposit a cat at the vet and you may think it is safe but you cannot possibly persuade yourself that the cat in such strange surroundings does not believe it has been deserted and has been left in a prison. There seems to be no answer except never to take a holiday.

Monty's big day in the dining-room window was Boat Race day. The Boat Race party, as far as we were concerned, came round each year much too quickly. An annual affair which had such raucous results as a Boat Race party, is apt to dissolve in some mysterious way with its predecessors. Time stands still. The guests have never left, or they are always just arriving or saying good-bye. Hence my old friends Mr and Mrs X are greeted by me at the door and I feel I am simultaneously greeting them this year, last year and the year before. Ours used to be a bottle party and as the Boat Race generally took place at some unearthly hour in the morning, guests began to arrive with their bottles at 9 a.m. The trouble with a bottle party is the stress it puts on the host and hostess who are inclined to greet their guests with graduated enthusiasm, according to the importance of the bottle. We had one guest who regularly brought a bottle of milk. I never found out whether this was a joke, for he consumed alcohol like everyone else; but I remember how our greeting became dimmer each year until it would have become extinct had we not departed for Cornwall.

The preparations, of course, began at the crack of dawn and as it was always a marathon day of festivity, large quantities of food were prepared to cope with late breakfasts, lunch, tea and those who still had the stamina to stay for supper. For Monty these preparations were a nuisance and this might be considered surprising because, with so much food about, one might have expected him to be the official taster. But he was never a greedy cat. He ate his requirements and no more, although like all of us he had certain favourite dishes, chopped pigs' liver, for instance, which he gobbled faster than others. He considered these preparations a nuisance, I think, because he wanted to get on with the party. He had a role to play, and it was a role which he enjoyed.

He would keep out of sight, the airing cupboard was the ideal hiding place, until he had the good sense to realise the towpath was waking up; shouts of small boys who without reason for loyalty to either University were violently partisan on behalf of one or other of the crews, odd couples booking places on the railings, then the appearance of hawkers with dark and light blue favours. There was a pleasant atmosphere of impending excitement, and it was now that Monty appeared and expected attention.

Both Jeannie and I were Cambridge supporters and before our first Boat Race party Jeannie had bought Monty a large light blue ribbon which she tied in a bow round his neck. I did not approve. I thought such a gesture was ostentatious and silly and I anticipated confidently that Monty would wriggle free from the encumbrance as soon as he had the chance. He did not do so. True the ribbon became more and more askew as the day wore on with the bow finishing up under his tummy, but this had nothing to do with any action on his part. It was the attention he received which caused that.

Hence the light blue ribbon became an annual ritual and invariably, after the bow had been tied, he would sit in the dining-room window staring with a lordly air at the crowds; and the crowds looking for a diversion until the race began would call to him and shout to their friends about him. He adored this period of glory. So much on his own but now at last receiving his due. And when our guests arrived, a hundred or more packing the cottage, a cacophony of laughter and talk, cigarette smoke clouding the rooms, people sitting on the floor and the stairs, glasses everywhere, Jeannie and I rushing around with bottles and plates of cold food, Monty was as cool as a cucumber. He would stroll from room to room, pausing beside a guest when the praise was high, even deigning to jump on a lap, ignoring the cat haters, refusing with well-bred disgust any morsel dangled before him by some well-meaning admirer. He was unobtrusively sure of himself; and when the rackety day was over, when Jeannie and I had gone to bed feeling too tired to sleep and we put out a hand and touched him at the bottom of the bed, we both felt safe. Safe, I mean, from the tensions among which we lived.

Sometimes I wonder if we would ever have come to

Cornwall had it not been for Monty. Decisions are often based on motives which are not obviously apparent, and cool intellects certainly would not believe that two people could change the mainspring of their life because of a cat. Such intellects, however, are free from turbulent emotions. They are the human version of the computer; to be envied, perhaps, because they are spared the distractions of light and shade. They can barge through life indifferent to the sensibilities of others because they have none themselves. Materialism in their view, is the only virtue.

Monty became a factor in our decision because he reflected, in his own fashion, stability. It did not matter how tired we were when we reached home, how irritated we might be by the day's conflict of personalities, how worried by inflated anxieties, how upset by apparent failures, Monty was solidly there to greet us. His presence, you might say, knocked sense back into us, He thus gave a clue to the kind of reward we might have if we exchanged our existing way of life for one that had a more enduring standard of values. We did not say this self-consciously at the time, too many other factors were involved; but on reflection I realise his example helped us to take the plunge.

The process of changing over from a city to a country life was spread over a year and more. We made several sorties to the cottage near Land's End during that time, and Monty was usually a companion. He appeared to be quite unconcerned by the

71

long car journey except once, and that was my fault.
I was naturally on guard against him jumping out of
the car in a panic whenever on the route I had to slow
down or stop; but there came a time when I exchanged
my ordinary car for a Land Rover. A saloon car you
could shut tight but a Land Rover with its canvas
hood had potential gaps through which a determined
cat might escape. I therefore bought him a basket
and at the instant of leaving Mortlake I pushed him
in it, banged down the lid and tied it, and set off.
It was an appalling miscalculation. Instead of ap-
preciating my action as a gesture towards his own
safety, he took it as an insult. He was enraged. He
clawed and spat and cried and growled. I was half
way to Staines when the noise of his temper forced
me to stop, and I gingerly lifted the lid up an inch. A
pair of eyes of such fury blazed through the slit that
I hastily banged down the lid again.

Now Jeannie was with me on this occasion and
inevitably this incident developed an argument. She
wanted to take him out of the basket. I was too scared
that once allowed to be free there would be no holding
him. My imagination saw him gashing us with his
claws as he fought to escape, then away like a madman
into the countryside. She, however, insisted that only
the basket angered him and he would be his old
gentle self as soon as he was let out. So the argument
went on, past Staines, past Camberley, past Basing-
stoke; it was not until we reached the outskirts of
Andover that I gave in. Monty was released and, with
a look of disgust in my direction the purrs began.

There was another occasion when he travelled as a stowaway on the night train from Paddington. Jeannie was always very proud of this exploit as she was the architect of its success. She was due to join me for the week-end and was dining at the Savoy before catching her sleeper when she suddenly decided she would like Monty to accompany her. She dashed back to Mortlake, found him, after a five minute desperate search, crouched on the wall at the end of the garden, and arrived at Paddington with three minutes to spare. Monty was an admirable conspirator. He remained perfectly still as she rushed him along the platform wrapped in a rug. Not a miaow. Not a growl. And nobody would ever have known that the night train had carried a cat, had Jeannie been able to curb her vociferous enthusiasm when she arrived at Penzance.

But she behaved as if the Crown Jewels were in her compartment. She was in such a high state of excitement when I met her that she did not notice the car attendant was directly behind me as she slid open the door to disclose her secret.

Monty's aplomb was superb. He stared at the man with regal indifference from the bunk. And as I recovered from my surprise and Jeannie muttered feeble excuses, all the car attendant found himself able to say was: 'Good heavens, what a beautiful cat!'

Five minutes later we were in the car on the road to Minack.

9

MONTY was wary in the beginning at Minack. He did not relax on those initial short visits, seldom put his nose outside the cottage, making even a walk of a few yards in our company a notable occasion. He was seven years old and needed time for readjustment.

Minack is a cottage a few hundred yards from the cliff and cupped in a shallow valley with a wood behind it. The walls grow up from great rocks which some crofter a few centuries ago decided would make the ideal foundation. The stones of the walls are bound together with clay and, when we first came, the floor inside the cottage was of earth layered over by thin boards. There are two rooms; one, which is the length of the cottage is our living-room and kitchen, the other a tiny one, is our bedroom; and there is a third room which we added as an extension along with a bathroom that became known in his lifetime as Monty's room. On one side of the cottage the windows stare out undisturbed, except for the old barn buildings, across moorland to the sea and the distant coastline rimming Mount's Bay; on the other, two small windows on either side of the door face a pocket of a garden. The old crofter, the architect of Minack, wished to defend the cottage against the south westerlies; and so this little garden, and the cottage, were set in the hill that rose away to the west. Thus, if we walk up the hill fifty yards and look back, the eye is level with the massive granite chimney; the chimney which to fishermen sailing back to Mousehole and Newlyn in a stormy sea gives the comfortable feeling they are near home.

There is no house or eyesore in sight; and this freedom amid such untamed country provides a sense of immortality. As if here is a life that belongs to any century, that there is no harsh division in time, that the value of true happiness lies in the enduring qualities of nature. The wind blows as it did when the old crofter lived at Minack, so too the robin's song, and the flight of the curlew, and the woodpecker's knock on an elm. This sense of continuity may be unimportant in a world with the knowledge to reach the stars; but to us it provided the antidote to the life we had led. It was a positive reminder that generations had been able to find contentment without becoming slaves of the machine. Here around us were the ghosts of men and animals, long forgotten storms and hot summer days, gathered harvests and the hopes of spring. They were all one, and our future was part of them.

Our plan was to earn a living by growing flowers and, the speciality of the district, early potatoes in pocket meadows on the cliff. We were, however, more influenced by the beauty of the environment than by its practical value; hence we presented ourselves with difficulties which had to be borne as a sacrifice to our whim. There was, for instance, no lane to the cottage. A lane ran from the main road a half mile to a group of farm buildings at the top of the valley; but once past these buildings it became rougher and rougher until it stuttered to a stop amid brambles and gorse. In due course we cut a way through and made a road, but in the beginning the nearest we could take the car to Minack was the distance of two fields; and across these two fields we used to carry our luggage . . . and Monty.

Jeannie on the first visit put butter on his paws. There had been a sad, remarkable case in a newspaper of a cat that had been taken away from his home near Truro to another near Chester from which he had immediately disappeared. Several weeks later he arrived back to his old Truro home but so exhausted and close to starvation that he died a day or two later. I do not pretend to believe this story, documented in detail as it was, but Jeannie did, and she had a vision of Monty dashing from Minack and making for Mortlake. Thus she used the old wives' recipe for keeping a cat at home by buttering his paws; the theory being of course that the cat licks off the butter and says to himself that such a nice taste is worth staying for. A slender theory, I think, though comforting.

But it was soon made clear on that first visit and repeated on succeeding ones that Monty had no intention of running away. It was the opposite that provided us with problems. He never had the slightest wish to leave.

During this period, as I have said, he distrusted the outside around the cottage, made nervous perhaps by the unaccustomed silence and the unknown mysterious scents; and when we urged him to come out with us, he would usually turn tail as soon as we dropped him to the ground and rush back indoors. He was, in fact, sometimes so timid that he annoyed me, and I would pick him up again, deliberately deposit him a hundred yards from the cottage, then, impotently, crossly, watch him race back again.

Why, then, did he always disappear when we were due to start back for Mortlake? The bags would be packed, one load perhaps already lugged across the fields to the car, and there would be no sign of Monty. Obstinately remaining inside the cottage when we wanted him to be out, he was now out when we wanted him to be in. But where? The first disappearance resulted in a delay of two hours in our departure for we had no clue where to look. He had no haunts to which he might have sneaked, because he had never been long enough out of the cottage on his own to find one; no haunts, that is, that we knew of. Yet apparently on one of his brief excursions he had made a note of the barn, and how at the bottom of the barn door was a hole big enough for him to wriggle through; and that as the barn at the time was not ours and the door was kept locked, and the key kept by a farmer ten minutes away, it was a wonderful place to hide in. It became a ritual for him to hide there at the end of each visit. The key fetched, the key returned, and in between I would have had to climb to a beam near the ceiling where Monty glared balefully down at me. Or was he saying: 'I like it here. Hurry up and make it my home?'

It became his home one April evening when the moon was high. We had now cleared a way through the brush of the lane and though the surface was too rough for ordinary cars, it was suitable enough for a Land Rover. On this particular evening we bumped our way along it, the canvas hood bulging with our belongings. Monty alert on Jeannie's lap, both of us ecstatically happy that at last the time-wasting preliminaries had been completed. We drew up with a jerk and I switched off the engine. It was a beautiful moment. No sound but that of the surf in the distance. The moon shimmering the cottage as if it were a ghost cottage. Here was journey's end and adventure's beginning. All we had worked for had materialised.

'Good heavens, we're lucky,' I said, then added

briskly as if to foreshadow the practical instead of the romantic side of our life to come, 'I'll get the luggage out . . . you go ahead with Monty and light the candles.'

But it was Monty who went ahead. He jumped from Jeannie's lap, paused for a moment to see she was ready to follow, then sedately led the way up the path. A confident cat. A cat who knew he was home. A cat, in fact, who was happy.

10

MONTY'S transition into a country cat was a gradual
affair. An urban gentleman does not become a
country gentleman simply by changing his clothes.
He must learn to adopt a new code of manners and a
new approach to the outdoors; to be less suave and
to show more bluster, to accept the countryside as a
jungle which has to be mastered by skill and experience. Monty, as an urban cat, had therefore a lot to
learn.

He first had to acclimatise himself to having us
always around and he showed his delight in various

ways. There was, for instance, the in-and-out window game, a game which was designed not only to display his affection but also to confirm his wonderment that we were now always present to obey his orders. Thus he would jump on a window sill and ask to be let out, only, a few minutes later, to be outside another window asking to be let in. This performance would continue for an hour until one of us lost patience, saying crossly: 'For goodness sake, Monty, make up your mind what you want to do.' He would then have the good sense to stop the game, replacing it probably by a short, though vigorous, wash.

There were the unsolicited purrs. A cat has to be in a very bad mood if a human cannot coax him to purr. There is little honour in this achievement, only the satisfaction that a minute or two is being soothed by such a pleasant sound. But the unsolicited purrs belong to quite another category. These are the jewels of the cat fraternity distributed sparingly like high honours in a kingdom. They are brought about by great general contentment. No special incident induces them. No memory of past or prospect of future banquets. Just a whole series of happy thoughts suddenly combine together and whoever is near is lucky enough to hear the result. Thus did Monty from time to time reward us.

My own preference was for the midnight unsolicited purr. For the first years, until we found a fox waiting for Monty to jump out, he had the freedom of the window at night. He used to go in and out and we were never disturbed if he chose to spend the night outside, perhaps in the barn. But when he did choose to remain indoors, and instead of settling on the sofa, preferred a corner of our bed, we felt flattered. It was then that I have relished, when sometimes I lay awake, the rich, rolling tones of an unsolicited purr.

In those early days the unsolicited purr was bestowed on us frequently. Later, when country life became to him a continuously happy routine it became rarer; but in the beginning the new pattern of his life was so ebulliently wonderful that he could not restrain himself. There he would be on the carpet in the posture of a Trafalgar lion and suddenly the music would begin. For no reason that we could see. Just his personal ecstasy.

There were other times when his show of affection was awkward. It was then that he posed a question that as a cat hater I used to find easy to answer, but now as a cat lover I found most difficult. How do you summon up courage to dismiss a cat who is paying you the compliment of sitting on your lap?

If you have a train to catch, if your life is governed by rules not of your own making, the excuse for removal is ready made. But in my case time was my own, the work to be done was the product of my own self discipline, I could not blame anyone else if I shoved off Monty who was comfortably enjoying a rest on my lap. I would gingerly start to lift him up, my hands softly encircling his middle, with the intention of placing him gently on the spot I was about to vacate; and he would hiss, growl and very likely bite my hand. True this was a momentary flash of temper with more noise than harm in it; but the prospect of its display, the certainty I was offending him, were enough time and again for me to postpone any action.

My subservience was made to look even more foolish when Jeannie, as she often did, served a meal on a tray. My seat was always the corner one of the sofa and so I used to endeavour to balance the plate-filled tray partly on the sofa arm, partly on Monty's back; trying, of course, to take great care not to put any weight on Monty. If, however, he showed signs of annoyance, if he woke up from his sleep and turned his head crossly round at me, I would edge the tray further over the arm so that it balanced like the plank of a see-saw. I enjoyed many meals this way in the greatest discomfort.

Rational people would not behave like that. I can imagine my own sneers if a few years before I had seen into the future and found I was going to behave in such a fashion. But there it was, I enjoyed it. I was glad to be of some service, and I used to be tinged with jealousy if he chose on occasions to honour Jeannie instead. Such occasions were rare because her lap was not up to his measurements. He overfilled it. He was like a large man on a small stool. She would sit, transfixed into immobility, and if at the time anything was being cooked in the oven it was sure to be burnt. Pleasure is relative to the desire of the individual. I do not know what pleasure Jeannie could have been offered in exchange for such moments with Monty.

These incidents may suggest that, now that the

three of us were always togther, Monty was spoilt. But is not a cat's nature, any cat, impervious to being spoilt? You can spoil a child and it can become a nuisance. You can spoil a dog and everyone except its owner is certain to suffer. A cat on the other hand, however luscious may be the bribes, remains cool and collected. Indulgence never goes to its head. It observes flattery instead of accepting it. Monty, for instance, did not consider himself an inferior member of the household; a pet, in fact. Thus he loathed it when condescension was shown to him; and many a misguided stranger trying to lure him with snapping fingers and 'pussy talk' has seen his haughty back. He was co-tenant of the cottage. He was not to be treated in that imbecile fashion so many people reserve for animals. The compliments he wished for were of the kind we gave him; we set out to implement any decision he made on his own by helping to make the result as successful as possible. We played the role of the ideal servants and we won our reward by watching his enjoyment. And there was another reward which Jeannie called 'paying his rent'.

His rent was making him do what he did not want to do. Hence this was the reward we forced him to give us when we felt in the mood to assert our authority. Jeannie might suddenly pick him up, hold him in her arms and hug him, when it was perfectly obvious that he wished to be left by himself. He would lie in her arms, a pained expression on his face, as she talked sweet nothings to him; and then, the rent paid, he would rush across the room to a window sill and sit there, tail slashing like a scythe, demanding to be let out.

I always maintained that Jeannie demanded more rent than I did. I think she had good reason to do so because she was responsible for his catering; and she was always filling plates or picking up empty ones or asking him to make up his mind what he wanted. 'Oh really, Monty,' she would say in mock fierceness, with Monty looking up at her as she stood by the sink, 'I've just thrown one saucer of milk away, you can't want another!' Or it might be one more morsel of fish required, and out would come the pan and down would go the plate.

His menu, now that we lived near a fishing port, was splendidly varied, and twice a week Jeannie would collect from Newlyn a supply of fresh fish. None of that shop-soiled whiting he used to have but sea-fresh whiting, boned megram sole or a little halibut or, what became his most favourite of all – John Dorey, the fish which fishermen themselves take home for their suppers. He would gobble John Dorey until he bulged, one of the few things which lured him to greed; and to satisfy this greed he would try to show his most endearing self to Jeannie. The spot where his saucers were placed was opposite the front door on the carpet at the foot of a bookcase which hid one corner of the sink. When he was hungry, a normal hunger not too demanding, he would sit on this spot, upright with front paws neatly together and the tip of his tail gently flicking them. His eyes would be half closed and he would sway imperceptibly to and fro. A meal was due but he was in no hurry.

Yet if John Dorey was on the menu and was simmering in a pan on the stove he could never restrain his impatience. He would walk excitedly up and down the room, roaring with anticipated pleasure, rubbing himself against Jeannie's legs, looking up at her as if he were saying: 'I love you, I love you.' Here was a cat who was no longer retaining his dignity. Nothing could hide the fact that at this particular moment Monty was thinking that Jeannie was the most wonderful cook in the world.

He would then have been ready to promise her, I am sure, all the rent she required.

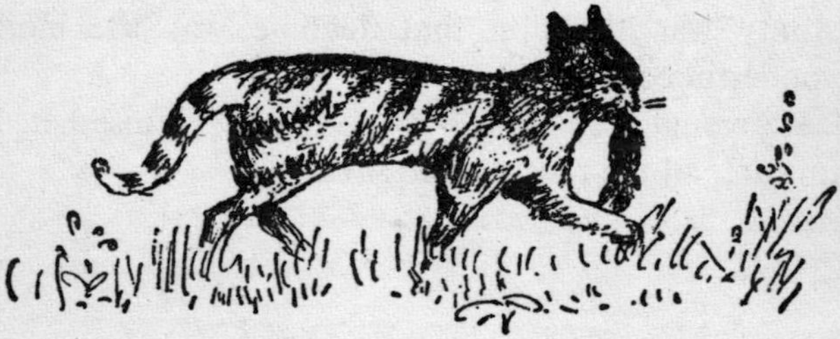

11

Monty's hunting at Mortlake had been limited to indoor mice, or indoor mice which happened to be outside. He soon began to find at Minack a variety of potential victims the like of which he had never seen before; and in some cases he was at a loss to the technique of attack required. I found him once, for instance, staring at a patch of ground under which a mole was digging.

My own first experience of a mole digging was the morning after a night out. It upset me. I was walking across a field, my head down, when I was

suddenly aware that a patch of soil the size of a hat
was moving. I stopped, stared and pinched myself.
The soil circled like a slow spinning top, rising upwards, the texture of a seed bed. Monty saw this for
the first time and was as startled as I had been. He
put out a paw as if he were thinking of touching a red
hot coal, then leapt backwards with a growl. 'It's
only a mole, old chap,' I said knowledgeably,
'only a mole digging a mole hill,' He was reassured
enough to advance again. He touched the soil with
his paw, then, meeting with no reaction, in fact finding
there was no danger or excitement for him at all, he
walked away with nonchalant composure; as cats do
when they suspect they have made fools of themselves.

Another puzzle for him was what to do when he
found an adder. A lizard, a slow worm or an ordinary
grass snake was an easy excuse for a few minutes play,
but an adder he sensed was a danger; and he was
certainly right. We have too many of them about. We
are always on guard during the summer wearing
Wellington boots whenever we walk through the
undergrowth; although it is in a warm spring when
they are at their most viperish. I have been happily
picking Scilly Whites on the cliff when I have suddenly
seen the poised head of one within a few inches of my
hand, hissing like escaped steam. In the summer they
will wriggle away as you advance towards them and
will whip up their heads and strike only if you step on
them or tease them. In the spring they will attack at
the slightest provocation and, as they have been
hibernating through the winter, the venom injected

into the wounds made by the fangs is a dose built up over the months. I learnt my lesson after the Scilly Whites, but Monty never learnt his lesson not to tease.

I have seen him touching the tail of an adder with his paw as if he were playing a dare game. It might have been even a form of Russian roulette because an adder can kill a cat, though this is very rare. As an adder is thirty inches long, perhaps he was deceived in to thinking that the head was too far away to catch him, or perhaps I was worrying unnecessarily. He certainly never was bitten by an adder, nor for that matter did he ever kill one. He flirted with the danger. It was a game . . . and yet, I wonder. There is a tradition in Cornwall that the capture and killing of an adder is the peak of a cat's hunting career; and when the rare victory is achieved the trophy is ceremoniously dragged whatever distance to the home and deposited on the floor of the kitchen for all to admire. Perhaps this was Monty's secret ambition. Perhaps above all he longed for the plaudits awarded to an adder killer. If so, the fates were against him.

I will not, fortunately, ever know the differences in flavour of mice — indoor mice, harvest mice, long tailed mice, short eared mice and so on. Shrews must be unpleasant because Monty, although he would catch them for fun, never ate them. But it seems obvious to me after watching the attitude of Monty that out-door mice have a far better flavour then the ordinary household mice. At Mortlake, he became, without being flamboyantly successful, a sound indoor mouse catcher. At Minack he spent so much time outside on the alert that often he lost the desire to fulfil his inside duties; and since the excitement of the chase should be the same both in and out, it occurred to me sometimes that the cause of his extraordinary behaviour may have been a bored palate.

I would be quite wrong to suggest that we were riddled with mice at Minack. For months we would be totally free of any sign of a mouse but at intervals one or two would arrive and cause us annoyance. They would make an unwelcome noise on the boards which provided our ceiling, and on occasions would descend to the sitting-room. Here Monty was often sleeping on the sofa. 'Monty!' I would say sharply, 'there's a mouse in the cupboard.' And Monty would go on sleeping.

The cupboard concerned was the shape of a large wardrobe, shelves climbing two sides while the back was the wall of the cottage. Apart from the china on the shelves with cups on hooks, there was a table in the cupboard on which stood a calor gas refrigerator; and under the table was the gas cylinder, pots and pans, a bread bin and various other household paraphernalia. Thus the cupboard was crowded and a mouse had a wonderful place to hide unless we set about clearing a space by removing the chattels into the sitting-room. We would perform this tedious task, then wake up Monty, carry him to the cupboard, and deposit him there. He was alone, except for the gas cylinder which was too much trouble to move, with the mouse.

Here, then, was a situation that was often repeated. Monty one side of the gas cylinder and the mouse on the other, and Monty had only to race once round the cylinder to catch it. Yet he would not budge. He would sit looking at me as if he were trying to tell me the mouse was his dearest friend. 'Go on, Monty!' my voice rising to a crescendo, 'go on, you ass. Catch it!' The mouse would move its position and I would push Monty towards it so that they met nose to nose. Still not a whisker of interest. Nor any sign of fear from the mouse. I would push and exhort and be angry and in the end give up in despair. Monty had a pact with the mouse and nothing I could do would make him break it.

But why? He was swift as a panther when outside. He would be across the land and into the hedge and back again with his capture inside a few seconds; and when necessary he had infinite patience. I always found it an endearing sight to look through the window and see him in the distance perched on a rock, staring intently at the grass a yard away; then begin to gather himself for the pounce, shifting the stance of his paws, swaying gently forwards and backwards, until he gauged the great moment had come. And when he missed, when by some miscalculation he ended up in the grass with his back legs spreadeagled and a waving tail denoting his failure, I sensed with him his disappointment. His successes, of course, were loudly trumpeted. He consumed his victims not at the place of execution but on a square yard of ground on the edge of the path leading up to the cottage. No matter how distant the capture he would return with it to this spot; and I would see him coming jauntily up the lane, a mouthful of grass as well as the mouse. A few minutes later when nothing was left he would let out the bellow of victory. 'Well done, Monty,' we would say, 'well done!'

He was a wonderful hunter of rabbits, and he had an earnest idea that these should always be brought into the cottage and left under my desk until I had seen them. This behaviour was prompted by my enthusiasm for the first rabbit he caught. It was a baby one and the incident took place within a month of his arrival at Minack; and because I was so anxious to see him settle down, my enthusiasm and that of Jeannie was far too vociferous.

I was writing a letter and never knew he had entered the room until I heard a soft jungle cry at my feet; and there was Monty, like a retriever, looking up at me with the rabbit beside him. He was inordinately proud of himself. He strode up and down the room as we praised him, with purrs loud enough for three cats, rubbing against us, then scampering back across the room to have another sniff. He never forgot the glory of this moment, and time and again we had to suffer a repeat performance. If we saw him coming we shut the door, and there was always plenty of time to do so. A rabbit was far too big for him to carry in his mouth, and he would pull it along on the ground. 'Poor rabbit,' Jeannie would say, dead though it was.

Monty never touched birds, except one when I saw him catch a wren which annoyed him. Wrens can be foolish and this one was foolish. They are so small that if they kept themselves to themselves no one need know their whereabouts; instead they proclaim their presence by the cross rattle of warning and, in spring, enjoy baiting any objects they dislike. There was Monty lying somnolent in the garden while a pair of Wrens rattled around him until he lost his temper and snatched one. I dashed forward, caught him, and put a hand to his mouth; and as I did so, he let the wren go and it flew safely away to a bush where it began its rattle again. And Monty went back to doze.

Monty's docile attitude to birds met its response from them. They showed no fear of him. It was I, if anything, who felt fear. I was always waiting for the incident that never happened.

12

I BECOME vague when I try to isolate the years. I
would like to have them arrayed in my mind in neat
compartments but I find instead they merge into
each other, and incidents connect themselves by
haphazard association rather than by dates. Thus the
flower seasons here at Minack, each of which has a
slow moving yet mounting dramatic entity of its own,
become dissolved in my mind into all flower seasons.
The hours I have crouched weeding anemones or
picking violets, lugging baskets of daffodils to the
packing shed, rushing the flower boxes in the
morning to Penzance Station, these hours do not

belong to one year but to all years. So also appear the storms that have battered Minack, and the lazy pleasure of hot summer days, the first scent of the may, the arrival of the chiff chaffs, the wonder of an angry sea with a fishing boat fighting for home. I have grown older not by passing each incident as if it were a milestone, but by being absorbed by them.

As Monty grew older his contentment was so obvious for all to see that we felt part of it. If something had gone wrong, if we had suffered some defeat which left us despondent, the sight of his magnificent person poised perhaps on some wall with the sun glinting his red bracken coat, his head alertly surveying the scene around him, would be enough to quell our momentary fears. His example was a positive contribution to the life we had chosen for ourselves.

I suppose it was this contentment that produced in him his calm attitude to birds. There was no need for him to kill for the sake of killing because he had so much else to do and, for that matter, so much else to think about. He was a great thinker. We have seen him so many, many times blinking away in the sun, not asleep, not awake, sitting upright with paws bunched, a shining white shirtfront, tail round his haunches, the tip flicking delicately. 'Look at Monty,' Jeannie would say, 'He's having his million and one thought.'

And while he was contemplating, the birds would be hopping around him. We had a bird table in the pocket garden opposite the front door and inevitably the crumbs we put on it used to be blown off on to the ground; neither Monty nor the birds were perturbed as they collected them. Of course if you live in the country you are certain to make friends with individual birds which respond to your approach with more trust than others. In our case we had two particular friends who hopped around Monty collecting the crumbs, whom we called Charlie and Tim.

Charlie was a chaffinch and Tim a robin, and they both treated Monty as if a cat was the most harmless thing in the world. Charlie was a bossy character who, in the spring and summer, used to follow us around cheeping all day. Even a bird's voice can sometimes sound too persistent and we used to chafe Charlie for the monotony of his cry. A gentleman chaffinch, if you look at it closely, is a beautiful bird. There is a touch of the tropics about its plumage of slate-blue, pink, chestnut, black and white wings and tail; only its voice is humdrum. Thus Charlie's voice as he perched on certain favourite places was a high pitched note repeated over and over again, until I marvelled sometimes that Monty was not irritated into action.

He would hop, for instance, at the entrance of the flower house while Monty was dozing on a bench and we were bunching the daffodils, piping away on and on until in exasperation I would say: 'For goodness sake, Charlie, think up another song.' Or he would perch on a certain stunted old apple tree under which in the lush grass Monty used to like to slumber; there would lie Monty curled in a ball while above him, with the monotony of a pneumatic drill, sang Charlie. But it was when we sat out of doors having breakfast or lunch that Monty was put most to the test.

We used to sit on a white seat, the scent of a verbena bush pervading the air, the sea in the distance, Monty at our feet, and Charlie a few yards away on the gravel path determinedly demanding crumbs from our plates. Nor would Charlie be alone, for he would have with him the dim little person who was his wife; and thus Monty had two to look at, to be tempted by, and yet to ignore.

In winter Charlie was a more silent individual, as if the summer had consumed his song. His feathers would lose their sheen, he would crouch rather than perch on a branch as if days were made to be borne instead of enjoyed. Sometimes he would disappear for weeks on end, and there was one winter when he was so long away that we made up our minds that he was dead. We missed his perky presence. We regretted our rudeness about his voice. We yearned to see his busy little nature once again. And we did. In the spring he suddenly appeared one day in the wood while Jeannie was feeding the chickens, the same old song, the same old Charlie, bossy as ever.

Tim was a gentle robin, if you can think of a robin as gentle. At least we ourselves never saw him attacking another or trying to assert his personality at the expense of other birds. Charlie would drive him off the bird table at any time. Tim simply did not

fancy a battle. He preferred to wait cunningly until
Charlie had had his fill, then he would return and
stay there until perhaps a tom tit would harshly tell
him to go; Tim, in fact, believed in appeasement.
This possibly was the reason why he liked so much to
be indoors with us, or in the flower packing shed when
we were there. He found life less troublesome, felt
safer, if he sat on corner of my desk, despite the fact
Monty might be wandering about the room. It was a
remarkable sight seeing Tim on the back of a chair
while Monty was on the chair itself. Or looking for
crumbs on the carpet while Monty lay stretched by the
stove. Or just flying around the room while Monty
appeared not to take the slightest notice. Of course,
Monty knew he was there. He observed Tim out of
the corner of his eye, but it was an eye that never had
the suspicion of a glint.

Yet Tim at times became so over-confident that he
seemed to be going out of his way to court attack
from Monty. I remember him once in the flower
packing shed standing delicately on one leg on the
cup of a daffodil that rose from a galvanised pail.
The pail was with others on the floor and there was
Monty threading his way between them until he
reached the spot where Tim was on the daffodil
looking down on him, while a paw stretch away he
was looking up at Tim; but neither bothered to show
any interest.

The height of Tim's foolishness was when he urged
his lady of the year to build a nest at ground level
among a bed of polyanthus. Heaven knows what

caused him to choose such a place because it was in an area fifty yards from the cottage which Monty had found a particularly fruitful hunting ground. Perhaps Tim had done so because it was so near to the packing shed, which meant he could have an idle time indoors without being too far from his mate. Anyhow I found the nest while I was picking the polyanthus, flushing the mate away as I did so.

At that moment, I saw Monty coming towards me, walking earnestly between two rows of plants, tail erect, a benign expression on his face which suggested that for some reason I was particularly popular. This was a moment to enjoy not to spurn, but I hastened towards him, swept him up in my arms and carried him, now cross, away to the cottage. Then I returned with bamboo sticks and a coil of wire netting and proceeded to encircle the nest in a cage. It looked safe when I had finished, but my activities had upset even Tim. The nest was never used again.

A third friend was Hubert the gull. He was far too superior, of course, ever to use the bird table, and he would stand on the rim of the roof waiting for us to throw food to him. Quite often Charlie would be there too, hoping to pinch a bite from under Hubert's beak; and Charlie would look ridiculous, so tiny beside Hubert yet so importantly awaiting us, that I used to call out: 'Charlie seagull is up on the roof!'

Our postman saw them up there together one day, and he told us the story of a seagull at Mousehole who paraded every day on a certain balustrade. A sparrow used to like it there too for visitors passed frequently by, and thus the sparrow and the seagull were regularly fed. One day, however, after the end of the season and the visitors had gone and food was no longer thrown to them, the gull suddenly eyed the sparrow, waddled quickly towards it, snapped it up and swallowed it whole. For a while after hearing that story we kept a watch on Hubert when Charlie was up there alongside him . . . just in case.

Hubert behaved towards Monty in his large way as Charlie and Tim did in their small way. Monty himself, at first was not sure of him. Hubert would sweep down from the roof, land on the path and advance towards Monty who retreated nervously looking round every few seconds and curling his mouth in a soundless snarl. I feel sure Hubert had no intention of attack. He was curious perhaps. He succeeded, however, in those first weeks after his arrival at Minack in establishing a moral superiority for a while over Monty:

Yet if a cat and a gull can like each other these two did, or at least they learnt to tolerate each other. I have seen them both on the flat rock that stretches out from one side of the cottage like a sacrificial stone, Monty at one end, Hubert at the other, and neither of them appeared to be perturbed.

Hubert never behaved so calmly when another gull arrived on the roof. The roof was his personal kingdom and if a gull swooped down and settled at one end, Hubert exploded in fury, half ran, half flew towards it, lunged out with his beak, then sailed into the sky in a storm of squawks chasing the offender this way and that until both disappeared over the fields towards the sea. A few minutes later he would return, fluff out his feathers and be at peace again as king of the roof.

There were times when Monty was certainly jealous of him. During those meals outside when Charlie and his squeak were ignored Monty would watch Hubert suspiciously as he stood with the presence of an eagle a little way off; and as soon as he began to come too close, Monty would advance timidly but surely until Hubert decided it was wise to retreat. But it was when Hubert accompanied us on our walks that Monty became most annoyed for he liked to have us to himself on these occasions and Hubert spoilt his pleasure.

Hubert would leave the roof as we set off down the lane, come swooping low over our heads, then up again into the sky, wheeling with the grace of a swallow; and when he came low again, his wings hissing the air with their speed, Monty would crouch and look up and glare. At other times we would be wandering around our meadows and fields with Monty trotting along with us when Hubert would dive from the sky, land on the ground twenty yards away, then strut on a parellel course; or if we had paused he would remain stationary, looking at us as if he were saying to himself, 'I wonder what they are up to?' These moments particularly infuriated Monty. He would begin to creep along the ground, stalking Hubert as he would a mouse, getting nearer and nearer, making a weird noise which was neither a growl nor a miaow. It was a comical sight. Both knew there would be no attack. Both knew the parts they had to play. It was a question of split second timing. As soon as Monty had arrived within a few feet, Hubert, to save him the embarrassment of coming any nearer, flew off.

In spring, Monty's thick coat began to moult and we used to give him a daily combing. He would lie on my lap as I traced the comb up and down his back, on his sides and up around the jowls of his neck. He loved it. He purred happily until I turned him over and began the same task on his underparts. There would now be silence except for a series of little grunts. He found it awkward to purr on his back.

And when it was all over I would collect the silky fur in my hand, go outside and throw it into the wind. It floated into the air soaring and billowing, eddying in the end to some thorn bush or tussock of grass or entangling itself in the sea pinks on the wall. It did not stay in any of these places for long. The fur was much sought after. Most nests around Minack were lined with it

13

As the years went by we became increasingly sensitive to the hazards that faced Monty. In the beginning we were so content with our new way of life that we foresaw the possibility of trouble neither for ourselves nor for him. Then, as the nature of our struggle became clear, we realised that we were going to have anxiety as well as contentment. The defeats and shocks we suffered, the lost harvest of daffodils, a field of beautiful anemones destroyed in a night by a southerly gale, a drought at a time when moisture for cliff potatoes was vital, brought home to us the extent of the battle in which we were engaged. Hence there were times when nervousness was substituted for calm and the foolish mood of anticipating trouble created unnecessary fears.

This foolish mood developed one evening at dusk when I saw an owl chasing Monty, diving at his up-turned startled face as if it were aiming to peck out his eyes. I rushed forward shooing it away, only for it to come back ten minutes later, and again the following evening, and the evening after that. I treated it as Monty's enemy, obsessed with the idea that it might blind him. 'That damn' owl is there again,' I would say, and hasten to frighten it away.

Jeannie's attitude towards it was quite different. She viewed my actions as utterly stupid and whenever I hurried to perform them she would crossly say: 'Leave it alone. It's perfectly harmless . . . It's *fond* of Monty.' This streak of romanticism had its origin in her childhood when she first came upon the rhymes of Edward Lear. A famous one had caught her fancy and she now saw the opportunity of watching its particular theme come to life.

The owl and the pussy cat went to sea
In a beautiful pea green boat.
They took some honey and plenty of money
Wrapped up in a five pound note.
The owl looked up to the stars above
And sang to a small guitar:
'Oh lovely pussy, oh pussy my love,
What a beautiful pussy you are, you are,
What a beautiful pussy you are.'

Nothing would shake her conviction that the owl pursued Monty out of a curious kind of affection; and I had to admit when several weeks had passed and no unpleasant incident had occurred that my fears were probably groundless. I refused to accept, however, that the owl *liked* Monty; and yet there were certain features of the relationship which were a puzzle. The tawny owls at Minack, and this was a magnificent tawny owl, nest at the top of the elms which surround a meadow close to the cottage. Very few cats could climb the specially favourite elm, and Monty was certainly not one of them. But the annual nest in this elm, just a cleft in the tree trunk, was a very foolish one and, usually, one or other of the nestlings would fall out. I would find one on the ground, a bundle of white feathers and two large unhappy eyes, and then laboriously climb up the tree and replace it beside its fellow. During this particular spring, however, I found no bewildered baby owl and as, later in the summer, I frequently saw the two sitting together like identical twins on various trees in the wood, it was clear no casualties had occurred. Hence Monty, against his nature and in a fit of madness, could not have climbed the elm and attacked the nest or killed a fallen nestling. He had, in fact, done nothing to incur the ire of the parent.

Yet there it was, the owl haunted him. It pursued him like a large dog with wings, swooping up and down as he walked innocently down the lane, cracking the evening air with its harsh cries of *kewick, kewick*. Nor would it leave him alone if he were happily

curled on a chair indoors. It wanted Monty to be out
with it. It would demand his presence by perching on
the wall outside the front door harshly repeating
again and again *kewick*, *kewick*. 'Didn't I tell you?'
Jeannie would smile and say. And I would reply
abruptly: 'For goodness sake don't be so whimsy.'

In the end I learnt to take the relationship for
granted. It went on throughout the summer and as I
never saw the owl make a direct attack on Monty
I lost my concern that it might do him harm. But
there was one incident which surprised me. I was
coming up the path from the cliff one evening when
there was still another hour or two of daylight, when
on turning the corner close to the cottage I saw the
owl perched on the back of the white seat. It stared
unblinkingly back at me, incongruous in such a
daylight setting as if it belonged to another world.
But what surprised me was that Monty was only a
few feet away, lying comfortably like a Trafalgar lion
in front of the seat. He saw me coming, got up and
stretched, and walked slowly forward; while the owl
heaved itself into the air and flapped off into the
wood. I felt as if I had disturbed two people having a
gossip.

I had other fears for Monty which were to prove
more tangible. He was too like a fox, for instance. I
did not appreciate this until a farmer one day came
hurrying up the lane to warn me he had seen a fox in
the field close to where we kept the chickens. It was
Monty, of course, a Monty with a burnished bracken
coloured coat which, I thereafter realised, certainly

did make him look like a fox. The same mistake was made at another time by a man with a gun whom I saw stalking beside the hedge which ran up from the wood. I charged across the field shouting at the top of my voice and when I reached the fellow, flustered and out of breath, he looked at me with disdain. He was about to shoot a fox. Up there in the corner where the winter gorse was in bloom. Can't you see it? Look it's moving . . . and Monty, alert at seeing me, came quickly through the grass towards us. These alarms put us on guard about the Hunt. The hounds might mistake Monty for their quarry and so when the Meet was at St Buryan or Lamorna Turn or anywhere else nearby, we used to keep him in all day.

But the hounds only once rushed through Minack and Monty was curled up on the bed at the time; and the reason we have been so lucky is that it is obviously dangerous for the hounds when they run for the cliff. Thus when a fox makes for our area the hounds are called off and the fox, sidling along the hedges of our fields to the impenetrable brambles and thorn trees which slope steeply to the sea, is safe. My instinct is always to be on the side of the fox. I suppose I have found that when one lives as we live, our daily existence posted like that of the ancient grey rocks which heave out of the untamed countryside everywhere around us, one is incapable of killing for sport. We share our life with the wild. We are part of it. Hence I will kill should an animal become an enemy, but never for fun.

Yet a fox, as everyone knows, can become an

113

enemy; and one summer when Monty was growing old, a fox's earth was found by a neighbour outside of which were the skeletons of four cats. The discovery thus explained why cats over a period of time had been disappearing from the homes of our neighbours, disappearances which hitherto had been blamed hopefully on the wandering instincts of farm cats. Then, two or three weeks later, a friend of mine saw a fox catch a cat. He saw the cat three fields away from where he was standing, intently looking at a point in the hedge, then poising himself for a jump, so full of concentration that it was deaf to the fox that was stalking through the grass behind it. My friend yelled at the top of his voice but the sound disappeared in the wind. He could do nothing but watch the fox pounce, then hurry away.

I do not believe that all foxes are cat-killers. You get a rogue which develops the taste for them, just as you get a rogue badger which brings calumny on his race by developing a taste for chickens; but whatever the case, whether one fox or two were guilty, a cat-killer was at large around Minack and Monty was in danger. We kept watch on him within the limit of ever being able to keep watch on the peregrinations of a cat; and although he did not usually wander far, he obstinately chose this period to do so. 'Have you seen Monty?' I would ask Jeannie, and when the answer was no we would forget the importance of what we were doing, and set out to search. We used to hasten around his known hide-outs, a dozen or so of which found favour in rotation, and when he was in none of these we were inclined to develop a panic.

On one such occasion I ran one way towards the sea and Jeannie another up the field towards the farm buildings at the top of the hill. When I rejoined her she had Monty in her arms, holding him tight and telling him what a fool he'd been. This is what had happened. She had reached the entrance to the field that faced our lane and was looking across the field to the far side when to her horror she saw a red object chasing another red object. She instantly guessed a fox was chasing Monty, and she began to run across the field calling his name; and she had run only a few yards when the second red object stopped and looked back at her. It was Monty. He was chasing a cub. Of course he did not know that it was running back to the earth where the cats were killed.

Soon after this we realised the killer was after Monty. We had proof of this one evening when we heard a fox barking as if on the doorstep followed by Monty flying in through the window. He plummeted at my feet and then turned glaring at the open window, growling. I ran to the door and out to the corner of the cottage which looks down the lane. I saw nothing and all I could do was to make a noise, the human version of an angry animal, which I thought would frighten the fox away. But Jeannie and I were now to behave extraordinarily foolishly.

We accepted the fact we had been stupid enough to allow him out at night without keeping him company, and so we decided from then onwards he would be kept indoors after dusk. Monty was furious. He had lived at Minack for six years and was over thirteen, and for the first time in his life he was forbidden the freedom of the night. He made such a hullaballoo, woke us up so often with his miaowing demands to be let out that three days later – and this was our foolishness – we gave in. 'All right, you go out,' I said, 'I'm not going to be kept awake by your fuss. I'm tired. I want to sleep. But you look out for that killer. He was after you last week. He'll be after you again.'

Our bed lay alongside the window so that if Monty was lying on it, then decided he wished to investigate what adventure awaited him outside, he had only to creep from the bedclothes to the sill and jump down on to the flower bed below. There he was tucked in on the bed when on the very next night after his freedom had been foolishly granted, he woke me up with the noisiest growl I have ever heard. I put out my hand and felt him creeping for the window. And then, from the daze of my sleep, I suddenly sensed there was danger. I grabbed Monty with one hand, and with the other found my torch. It was a torch with a new battery; and when I shone it out of the window I saw a magnificent sight.

A fox, the size of an Alsatian. At first directly beneath the window sill. Then gliding away down the lane, so silently, so superbly a thoroughbred that for a moment I forgot he was a killer and I called out to Jeannie:

'Quick! Wake up! You'll never see such a beautiful fox!'

And up to now, I have never done so again.

14

THERE were other hazards beside foxes; and there are two episodes in Monty's life at Minack that I would like to forget, but which remain painfully in my mind. Yet, and this is the paradox, I like also to remember them because of the happiness which followed, that magical sense of happiness when someone you love is reprieved.

The first took place the year before myxamatosis swept the rabbits away from our area, and when the gin trap was still the method used for their elimination. Such was our isolation at Minack that the fields where the traps were set were in a ring around us; and we were so far from other habitations that we alone suffered the hell of the traps' successes. We heard the momentary screams and the silence which followed. We lay in bed awaiting the next anguished cry, as we awaited once the next stick of bombs. A long way away those who were responsible for setting the traps would be pursuing their evening enjoyment while Jeannie and I, as if in the midst of a battle, listened.

A chill went through us whenever we heard the signal of traps being laid, the metallic sound of the trapper's hammer; and if Jeannie heard it first she would run looking for me, and we would both then go looking for Monty. I admit that rabbits had in some way to be controlled but it was the manner in which gin traps were used which was so barbarous. It was seldom that any steps were taken to cut short the pain of the trapped. The traps, set perhaps an hour before dusk, reaped most of their harvest in the first half of the night as the rabbits came out of their burrows. The screams then followed each other as if they were an endless series of echoes and we would have little time to remain tense, waiting for the next; but after midnight we had to wait, ten minutes, half an hour, or suddenly two or three, one after the other, then silence. It was not often that anyone considered it humane to come at midnight and kill those caught during the evening flush. We had to lie there thinking of them.

It was late one lovely May afternoon that Monty

got caught in a trap. We knew that traps had been laid in the field adjoining the cottage but traps were not supposed to be actually set until dusk; and thus Monty should still have had an hour or two in which he could have wandered around in safety. Nevertheless we were nervous for him. We were in the mood to anticipate trouble and I said to Jeannie: 'I don't think we ought to let Monty out of our sight for an instant this evening.' There seemed to be no reason why we should. Our day's work was ended and we were both pottering about the garden and the cottage while Monty was in one of his benign moods. He was lying half-hidden among the wall-flowers outside the front door, blinking sleepily, as if he were relaxing after a large meal. He was the epitome of contentment, a much loved, magnificent ginger cat who was at peace with his private world; and heaven knows what prompted him suddenly to go somewhere he had never been before.

Unseen by us, he left his nest under the wall-flowers, entered the field where the traps were laid and walked the length of it, miraculously threading his way through the traps until he was caught by one at the far end, close to a gap in the field which led down to the cliff.

I do not think five minutes had elapsed before I noticed his absence from the garden; and instinctively I knew what had happened. I shouted to Jeannie to follow me, then ran the few yards to a bank which rose above the field. I stood on it for an instant while my eyes peeled along the base of the hedge where the traps were set. I saw nothing but young green corn; until suddenly in the far distance I saw an object at ground level languidly flopping up and down. It was Monty's tail.

The next twenty minutes are a jumble in my memory. We raced across the field, enraged that our care for him had cheated us; and when we reached him and saw his yellow eyes looking trustingly up at us while his little front paw with the white smudge on it was squeezed in the gin, we broke out with curses against those responsible for setting it.

'I'm going to throw it away!' Jeannie cried, 'right away in the sea.' But this outburst did not help us release Monty. He began to struggle so I put my hands firmly round his body while Jeannie tried to open the gin; and as only a few weeks before she had released a trapped dog she could not understand why, on this occasion, the fangs had stuck fast. Poor Monty; sweat began to moisten his fur and his mouth frothed, and then panic seized him and for an instant he freed himself from my hold.

'Look out!' I shouted. He lashed out with his three free legs, claws like spikes, too quick for Jeannie to move away in time and I saw a line of blood on her arm. A second later he was quiet again, lying panting on his side, tongue lolling, uttering little cries, and his paw still trapped.

I do not wish to remember again the ten minutes which followed. A hideous time against the background of a sea-scented evening, larks exultant in the sky, early swallows skimming in from the south, the pilchard fleet chugging out into Mount's Bay. I do not wish to remember the anguish of those ten minutes; only the sweet relief we had when at last we had him safe. He lay exhausted for a while on the sofa while Jeannie tried to tempt him with warm, sugared milk and we angrily discussed what we should do.

The trap would go into the sea. I would make a complaint. We both, in fact, blistered with fury; and yet, maddeningly enough, there was nothing we could righteously be furious about. We did not possess the field concerned, and so Monty, in the legal sense of the word, was trespassing. Thus the whole incident revolved around the question of standards. The countryman had grown up to expect a layer of cruelty in his life. We had not. Thus when Jeannie threw the trap away and I made my angry complaint, it was inevitable that a feud should begin. We did not mind of course. We at least had proclaimed our indignation against cruelty. And in any case the vet had seen Monty. No permanent harm had come to his paw.

The other episode took place when he was fourteen years old. We now had a splendid greenhouse a hundred feet long and twenty feet wide, and during this particular winter we were growing sweet peas for early spring flowering. We spent hours of our time pinching them out and layering them and it was only natural that Monty should be with us during these sessions. He amused us while we pursued the monotonous task. For no reason at all he would race up and down the rows or ridiculously treat a sweet pea tendril as an enemy, or interrupt the flow of our work by turning upside down at our feet requesting his tummy to be tickled. There were no signs that he was an old cat. He looked in magnificent condition and when one day we put him in a basket which hung on the potato scales, he weighed eighteen and a half pounds net.

Yet there were a couple of incidents during the daffodil season – it begins with us late in January and ends according to the warmth of the spring in the latter part of March – that made us puzzle about him. On each occasion he appeared momentarily to stagger and yet so briefly that it could have been an accidental lack of balance and not a signpost to coming illness. In between times he was completely normal, the usual large appetite and as agile as ever.

Then one day at the end of March we went out and did not return till after dark; and as so often happened, the headlights as we came up the lane to the cottage lit up his fierce face as he glared at us from the bedroom window. He had the gift of making us feel we had neglected him. It was an echo of those late Mortlake nights. 'Where have you been?' he seemed to be crossly saying.

On this occasion we performed the inevitable rites of apology, picking him up and hugging him, and hastening to bribe him to return our affection by the obvious method of filling his plate with fish. Jeannie had turned to the sink to collect the fish pan when I suddenly saw Monty begin to stagger and half stumble across the carpet to a spot under my desk, where he collapsed.

'Look at Monty!' I shouted, and rushed over and knelt beside him, stroking him; and because I met with no response, his eyes seemed to be glazed and unseeing, I picked him up and carried him to our bedroom. He was desperately ill.

'You stay here,' I said to Jeannie, not certain whether I was asking her to carry out the best or the worst of the two tasks, 'while I race up to the farm and telephone the vet. If he's in he'll be here within half an hour.' And miraculously he was in and, within half an hour he was at Minack. We both looked at his face as he carried out his examination, seeking to read the signs we hoped to see. 'Is it a heart attack or a stroke?' I murmured, fearing his answer.

He was a quiet Scot with the comforting assurance of his race; and goodness knows why but I always prefer it when advice comes in a Scot's accent. 'I don't think so,' he said slowly, 'you see his eyes are rolling, and look how he's struggling.' He paused for a moment. 'You haven't been putting any poison down, have you?' I hadn't, but I suddenly remembered the sweet peas and the dust we had been using on them to check disease, and I rushed out into the night to find the tin. I brought it back and the vet slowly read the instructions and list of chemical ingredients.

'That's the trouble all right,' he said, 'he's been poisoned though there's no mention here the dust is dangerous. The fact is he's absorbed the dust in his fur and body over the months and now he's got enough inside to hit him.'

He was in a coma for two days and nights. He lay on the pink bedspread in the spare bedroom while one of us sat always with him. The treatment was bicarbonate of soda every four hours and as it required both of us to pour the dose down his throat the one who was on night duty woke up the other when the fourth hour came round. About six o'clock on the second morning we had carried out our duty and we were standing together watching him . . . and suddenly there was a purr.

'Oh Monty Monty!' cried Jeannie, 'you're safe. You're safe!'

For us the remaining year of his life had the delicate pleasure of borrowed time.

15

In previous years we had occasionally to go away, never for more than three or four days, and elaborate arrangements of course were made for Monty's welfare. A travelling fish salesman supplied fish from his van, and whoever it was we had helping us at Minack at the time would cook it, and keep a saucer filled with milk from the farm. Monty was allowed to wander about as he liked during the day but in the evening he would be locked indoors; and when we were going to bed three hundred miles away in London, there was comfort in the thought he was safely ensconced within the cottage. We hated leaving him and he in his turn throughly disapproved of our absence; and on one occasion he nearly made us miss our train.

We were going by night, and while in the afternoon Jeannie was packing, he sniffed around the suitcases in that apprehensive fashion that both dogs and cats are apt to show when travel is scheduled. He then quite suddenly began to limp. I had never seen him limp before but there he was hobbling about as if he had only three legs. This continued for an hour; and so theatrical were his gestures that Jeannie declared she would not catch the train unless he was seen by the vet. The vet was fetched and he pronounced Monty a malingerer. There was nothing wrong with him at all; and Monty, admitting his bluff had been called, promptly began walking normally again.

Our returns usually had a chilly reception. He liked at first to pretend that he could get on perfectly well without us and it was immaterial whether we lived at Minack or not. The pretence lasted until we went out for a stroll to see how things had been growing while we had been away; and as we walked we would suddenly hear a bellow of a miaow, then see Monty running towards us. We would continue our stroll with him at our heels, while at intervals the bellow was repeated. It was a touching experience for in the sound was the agony of loneliness. We knew then how much he had missed us.

But in the last year of his life there was no need to go away, and although sometimes we were absent during the day we were always with him at night. He recovered splendidly from the dust poison, and by the early summer he was his usual beautiful self. 'Oh, what a beautiful cat!' some hiker would say as he passed through Minack seeing Monty perched aloofly on a stone. 'How old is he?'

No one believed he was nearly fifteen. Nor did I for that matter. Time deceives in its pace, luring years into yesterdays, garlanding memories without intervals, seeping the knowledge of age into one's mind. I did not want to say how old he was. I did not want to remember that for so long he had been the recipient of our secret thoughts. Each of us had talked to him in that mood of abandon which is safe within friendship. Maybe it was only a cat's friendship, but secure never to be tarnished, easing problems because the aftermath of confession did not breed the fears of disclosure.

He was an integral part of our failures and successes at Minack, and a hulky miner from St Just whom we once had helping us called him the foreman. 'Look out, the foreman's coming,' he would shout as he lunged away with his shovel in a potato meadow, 'we'll get our cards if we don't do our job properly.' Monty would appear and walk leisurely down the row where he had been digging, sniffing the discarded potato tops which spreadeagled on the side as if he were checking that all the potatoes had been collected from the plants. It was always a solemn inspection. There were no games. And when he had completed it, and had left the meadow, disappearing

131

out of sight, the hulky miner would stab his shovel into the ground, rub his hands together and call out: 'All clear boys. We can have a smoke now.'

He was sometimes an inconvenience when we were picking flowers. At daffodil time the pace of picking has to be so fast that there is no time for distractions; and yet Monty would often insist on accompanying us, walking ahead between the daffodil beds at a very slow pace of his own choosing so that our feet tumbled over him. 'Hurry up, Monty,' I would say, but at the same time I did not want to sound too brusque. I was glad that he wished to be with us; and so I would stop the rhythm of my picking and bend down and stroke him. Then, if he did not move, I would step over him.

He had a passion for violet plants and, in his time, we used to grow three or four thousand every year. The variety was called Bournemouth Gem and each plant bushed dark green leaves that perfumed the meadow in which they were grown even before the violets themselves appeared. Monty liked rolling among them. The rich orange of his fur against the dark green was a pretty sight and although you would have expected him to do damage, little damage was done; the plants were such fat cushions that the few broken leaves had plenty waiting to replace them. So we let him roll and only became alarmed when he jumped on a plant, gathered as much of it as he could with his four paws, turned on his side, and proceeded furiously to disembowel it. The fact is he liked the smell of violets. I have often seen him walking on his own down a row, his tail pointing like a periscope above the leaves, smelling the plants on either side of him. 'Monty's picking violets,' I would say to Jeannie as a joke.

He enjoyed sitting on the bench in the packing shed hemmed in by galvanised tins of wallflowers or jars of violets or anemones. He would sandwich himself in a space and if you looked in from the outside you would see through the window a splendid array of early spring flowers and in the midst of it all the dozing face of Monty. I remember a flower salesman coming to see us one day who was so amazed by what he saw in the packing shed that he nearly forgot to discuss his business; for there was Monty among the daffodils, and Tim the robin up on a shelf warbling a song from a jar of anemones, while Charlie the chaffinch was looking up at us calling his monotonous note from the floor. These three had three flower seasons together and this particular occasion was the last. First Monty, then Tim eighteen months later, and Charlie six months after that. And all the while up there on the roof was Hubert, observing everything, majestic, so compelling a character that neither of us would dare to let him remain hungry if he were demanding a meal, however busy we might be. 'Jeannie!' I would call out as I was stacking flower boxes in the Land Rover ready for Penzance Station, Hubert's hungry. Have you got anything?'

Monty was always tempted by boxes. If a parcel arrived and Monty was in the room and we unpacked it, he was certain to fill the vacant space. Perhaps he was born in one. Perhaps a psychiatrist would be right in saying that parcels and cardboard boxes recalled exquisite incidents of kittenhood. He certainly loved flower boxes and the tissue paper we put in them; and many a time we used to relieve the intensity of our work by pretending Monty, lying in a flower box, was indeed a flower. 'Shall we send him to Covent Garden?' one of us would say absurdly. 'They'd certainly call him a prize bloom,' the other would reply equally absurdly. When we were working at great pressure, it was a relish to have Monty to distract us, in so kind and pleasant and trivial a way.

16

ONE of Monty's lovable characteristics was the way he enjoyed going for walks with us, trotting along like a dog at our heels. Sometimes when we wanted to go on a proper walk, a walk far longer than he could manage, we would sneak down the path planning to get out of sight without him realising we had gone; but from some hide-out in which he was spying upon us, he would suddenly appear, all smiles as if he were saying: 'Going for a walk? Good idea, I'll come too.' Then, of course, we had to cancel our plans and go on a limited walk instead.

He played games on these walks, some of which were vexing, some charming. He had the usual whim of a cat to tear up trees as if the wind were in his tail, but as many of the trees were elders he never climbed high. It was at night that these climbs were annoying.

We would be taking a late night stroll and wishing to return to go to bed when he would race up the elder which is opposite the old barn and obstinately stay there. My voice would at first sound coaxing, then commanding, and then frankly I would lose my temper. 'Come on, Monty, come down!' I would shout at him. He would not budge so in the end, with Jeannie standing beside me holding the torch, I would climb the tree towards the pair of phosphorescent eyes which stared down from above. I would be up there among the branches trying to grab him, while Jeannie was laughing at both of us in the darkness below.

He had an endearing game he played when he thought a walk required livening up; or perhaps because he decided we were not giving him enough attention. He would wait until we had gone several yards ahead of him, crouching meanwhile on the path and shifting his paws as if he were about to spring . . . and then race at terrific speed up to and past us, coming to a full stop a couple of yards away. Thereupon we inevitably bent down and made a fuss of him. Then we would go on, and soon the game would be repeated.

The longest walk he used to take was to the Carn we can see from our windows at Minack and which stands above a cascade of rocks that fall to the sea below. It is a rough walk most of the way, a track through gorse and brambles and bracken while on either side of a long stretch of it there is a whole series of badger sets. In spring time the land around is sprayed with bluebells while may trees plume white from among them; and ahead is the Carn and the panorama of Mount's Bay.

We used to make it an early morning walk when the dew was still wet on the grass, and a peaceful one if Monty was in a docile mood; but there were times when we would pass the badger sets thinking he was behind us, and suddenly find he had disappeared down one of the cavernous holes. It would take us a few minutes before we found which hole he had chosen, then we would see him looking up from the dark, just out of reach. I found myself thinking on these occasions he was taking a mischievous revenge on the only time I ever had power over him . . . when he wanted me to open a door or a window; for there he would be holding up the walk, and nothing we could do except await his decision to rejoin us.

His favourite walk, or stroll I should call it, was fifty yards down the lane to the stream; a stream which rushed water from November to June, then dried up and became a dip in the roadway. It was a stroll that now has a significance for Jeannie and myself because it represents in our memories the joy of his first stroll and the sadness of the last.

The first night on which we came to live at Minack the moon was high, and after I had transported our luggage to the cottage, we celebrated the freedom we had captured by taking this stroll. The moon was shining, except for the murmur of the sea and the hoot of owls, on silence.

Monty, who in the first week or two was going to be shy in daylight, came with us, nosing his way down the lane which to him was full of imaginary dangers, sniffing, hesitating, taking no action except to advance steadily towards the sparkling water that ribboned ahead of him. And when at last he reached it and put out a paw in puzzlement I felt this was an occasion when I must not allow him to have any further apprehension; and so I bent down to pick him up and carry him over. He was quick to expose my foolishness. He slipped from my hold, and with the grace of a gazelle he leapt the stream. From that moment, this miniature valley across the lane has been called Monty's Leap.

It was in daffodil time that his illness began to threaten the normality of his days. Nothing sudden, no pain, just a gradual ebbing of strength; so that first the bluebell walk to the Carn had to be abandoned, then the one we used to take along the top of the cliff, and then even the strolls to the Leap became less frequent. I would watch him from the corner of the cottage wending his way down the lane, and my heart would yearn to see a spring in his movements I knew I would never see again. He would reach the stream, drink a little, then turn and come slowly

back. This stroll was the yardstick of our hopes, and
sometimes Jennie would come running to me: 'He's
been twice to the Leap this morning!' . . . and her
voice would have the tone that the inevitable was going
to be defeated.

But I knew sooner than Jeannie that there was
nothing we could do, nothing that her loving care
and nursing ever could achieve. Each time I saw him
set off for the Leap I was on guard; and there was one
evening, the last evening, when on seeing him, from
our window, start down the lane we ran to follow
him only to find that after a few yards he had lain
down. Then on a few yards and down again; and yet
he was such an old warrior that when I picked him
up he tried weakly to struggle free . . . as if he were
saying: 'Let me be, I can make it!' I gently gave him to
Jeannie to take home to the cottage, and as I watched
her I realised that she too now knew that our life
with him was over.

He died on a lovely May morning in his sixteenth
year. I had hurried to fetch the vet and on my return I
found Jeanie had taken him out into the warm sun
and he was breathing gently on a bed of lush green
grass. Up above on the roof was Hubert, quite still,
his feathers bunched, as if he were waiting for something; and within a yard or two of Monty were his
friends, Charlie and Tim. No sound from either of
them. Tim on a rosebush, Charlie on a grey rock.
They were strange mourners for a cat.

The next day, soon after the sun had risen above
the Lizard far away across Mount's Bay, we carried

him down the lane to the stream and buried him beside it. Between his paws we placed a card:

Here lies our beloved friend Monty who, beside the stream that crosses the lane and is known as Monty's Leap, is forever the guardian of Minack.

DEREK TANGYE
THE AMBROSE ROCK

There must be legions of people who yearn to pack up
their jobs and find some patch of land where they can
settle down and create their own 'earthly paradise'.
Jeannie and Derek Tangye are among the lucky few
who have done just that. They have succeeded in
turning a dream into a reality at Minack, a flower
farm on the wild and beautiful coast of Cornwall.
Today, Derek Tangye's heartwarming chronicles of
life away from it all are known and loved all over the
world. His delightful stories of Minack and the
creatures who share his life there not only re-create
the magic and beauty of the very special world that he
and Jeannie have created, but also impart something
of the very spirit of Cornwall.
THE AMBROSE ROCK, Derek's latest book, tells
the enchanting story of Ambrose the cat since the loss
of Oliver – his partner in crime. Ambrose's exploits at
home and away make delightful reading and give you
a glimpse of the very special world of Jeannie and
Derek Tangye.

AUTOBIOGRAPHY   0 7221 8394 1   **£1.50**

Also by Derek Tangye and available in Sphere paperback:
LAMA   A CAT AFFAIR
SOMEWHERE A CAT IS WAITING   THE WAY TO MINACK
A DONKEY IN THE MEADOW   THE WINDING LANE
SUN ON THE LINTEL   COTTAGE ON A CLIFF
WHEN THE WINDS BLOW

A selection of bestsellers from SPHERE

FICTION

FULL CIRCLE	Danielle Steel	£2.25 ☐
SUMMER SONG	Pamela Oldfield	£2.25 ☐
THE AMTRAK WARS VOLUME 2:		
FIRST FAMILY	Patrick Tilley	£2.25 ☐
DELCORSO'S GALLERY	Philip Caputo	£2.25 ☐
THE BRITISH CROSS	Bill Granger	£1.95 ☐

FILM & TV TIE-INS

THE RIVER	Steven Bauer	£1.95 ☐
INDIANA JONES AND THE LOST		
TREASURE OF SHEBA	Rose Estes	£1.25 ☐
THE WHALE TALE	John Stevenson	95p ☐
BEST FRIENDS	Jocelyn Stevenson	£1.50 ☐

NON-FICTION

EDWINA	Richard Hough	£2.95 ☐
KITTY CAMPION'S HANDBOOK OF		
HERBAL HEALTH	Kitty Campion	£2.95 ☐
TALKING TO MYSELF	Anna Raeburn	£1.95 ☐
A JOBBING ACTOR	John Le Mesurier	£1.95 ☐
AROUND THE WORLD IN 78 DAYS		
	Nicholas Coleridge	£1.95 ☐

All Sphere books are available at your local bookshop or newsagent, or can be ordered direct from the publisher. Just tick the titles you want and fill in the form below.

Name _____

Address _____

_____

Write to Sphere Books, Cash Sales Department, P.O. Box 11, Falmouth, Cornwall TR10 9EN

Please enclose cheque or postal order to the value of the cover price plus:

UK: 55p for the first book, 22p for the second book and 14p for each additional book ordered to a maximum charge of £1.75.

OVERSEAS: £1.00 for the first book plus 25p per copy for each additional book.

BFPO & EIRE: 55p for the first book, 22p for the second book plus 14p per copy for the next 7 books, thereafter 8p per book.

Sphere Books reserve the right to show new retail prices on covers which may differ from those previously advertised in the text or elsewhere, and to increase postal rates in accordance with the PO.